CREATIVE SILENCE

CREATIVE SILENCE

KEYS TO THE DEEPER LIFE

J·E·A·N·I·E   M·I·L·E·Y

WORD PUBLISHING
Dallas · London · Sydney · Singapore

CREATIVE SILENCE: KEYS TO THE DEEPER LIFE

Scripture quotations used in this book are from the following sources:

The King James Version of the Bible (KJV).
The New American Standard Bible (NASB), © 1960, 1962, 1963, 1968, 1971, 1972, 1973, 1975, 1977 by The Lockman Foundation. Used by permission.
The Holy Bible, New International Version (NIV). Copyright © 1973, 1978, 1984 International Bible Society. Used by permission of Zondervan Bible Publishers.
The New Testament in Modern English (PHILLIPS) by J. B. Phillips, published by The Macmillan Company, © 1958, 1960, 1972 by J. B. Phillips.
The Revised Standard Version of the Bible (RSV), copyrighted 1946, 1952, © 1971, 1973 by the Division of Christian Education of the National Council of the Churches of Christ in the U.S.A., and are used by permission.
The New Testament in the Language of the People (WILLIAMS) by Charles B. Williams, copyright 1949 by Moody Press.

Library of Congress Cataloging-in-Publication Data

Miley, Jeanie.
Creative silence: keys to the deeper life / Jeanie Miley.
    p.   cm.
Bibliography: p.
ISBN 0-8499-0667-9
1. Prayer—Christianity.   2. Meditation—Christianity.   I. Title.
BV215.M48   1989
248.3—dc19   88-27245
                                                                      CIP

Printed in the United States of America
9 8 0 1 2 3 9 BKC 9 8 7 6 5 4 3 2 1

To
my parents,
Dr. and Mrs. Louis D. Ball,
who introduced me to Christ
and taught me to pray,

my husband,
Martus Miley,
whose quiet strength has shown me the presence of Christ,
and who has blessed my creativity,

my daughters,
Michelle, Julie, and Amy,
who have been a source of delight and inspiration.

To these human instruments of
God's gracious love,
thank you.

CONTENTS

FOREWORD

Oliver Wendell Holmes observed astutely that "many people go to their graves with their music still in them."

This is a book for the Christian that opens up the possibilities for the music to be released into the world now and heard in the day-to-day nitty gritty routines of life. Each of us as people of God has a deep yearning to experience a profound inner relationship with the Lord. But, unfortunately, we become so involved in the razzle dazzle of striving and doing that it is easy to get sidetracked into constantly *doing* instead of *being*.

It is as hard for us to get our priorities straight as it was for the prophet Elijah almost three thousand years ago. *The Bible in Today's English Version* describes his experience on Mount Sinai when he desperately needed reassurance from God, "Then the Lord passed by and sent a furious wind that split the hills and shattered the rocks—but the Lord was not in the wind. The wind stopped blowing, and then there was an earthquake—but the Lord was not in the earthquake. After the earthquake there was a fire—but the Lord was not in the fire. And after the fire there was the soft whisper of a voice"—and it was then that Elijah recognized that the soft whisper of a voice was the Lord (1 Kings 19:11).

It is that "soft whisper of a voice" that we long to hear. But to really hear, we must know how to listen. And listening is an active art that is not stumbled onto willy nilly, but is acquired through persistent and prayerful effort. It is indeed an important key to moving into the realms of the deeper spiritual life so that the music inside each of us can be released to bless and benefit others.

In *Creative Silence*, Jeanie Miley has given us a practical and sensitive guide to an understanding of how to penetrate the marvelous mystery of God's presence, even in the earthquakes and wind and fire and noise of daily living. For it is not until we get beyond these that we are able to hear the "still small voice" of the Lord.

As you read these pages, I believe you will be gently nudged, as I have been, toward a clearer understanding of the gift of prayer and meditation as a release for our spirits that allows them to soar into the rarified atmosphere of God's presence. Three hundred years ago a French spiritual leader by the name of Francois Fénelon expressed the idea that it was quite likely to be harder for a person in business or in the professions to meditate and pray than for a cloistered monk—*but it was far more necessary.* Certainly the distractions of twentieth century living only further accentuate Fénelon's observation!

Then, too, I'm sure many of us can identify with the author's friend who is quoted as knowing the anguish of keeping "all of the rules and missing out on the joy." In *Creative Silence*, we find tried and tested techniques that will enable us to wrench free from our squalid efforts at rule-keeping and to become joy-filled Christians who season society around us with a faith that works in our chaotic and noisy world.

While not in the least autobiographic, Jeanie Miley rolls back the curtains of her own experiences and feelings in a way that is remarkably easy for us to identify with. It helps to know that someone else has felt the way we do in our common struggle to be practical Christians—to be "in Christ."

I am especially attracted to the exercises that accompany each chapter. To some of us, it may seem a bit strange to undertake the step-by-step disciplines suggested. But I suspect that once we've overcome any self-consciousness we may feel, we'll be amazed at our newly discovered release as we encounter a living Lord who is on our side and will move us gently each day into new experiences of His grace and love.

FLOYD THATCHER
General Editor,
Guideposts
Home Bible Study Program

INTRODUCTION

The sixth chapter of Mark tells of a stormy night when the men who had followed Jesus around were scared. Although the fishermen strained at their oars in the darkness, trying in vain to get control of their boat, giant waves continued to toss their boat about.

Jesus came to His friends, walking through the storm, and sat down in the middle of their troubling circumstances. In His presence and at His word, the waters stilled, and there was peace.

Life at the end of this twentieth century often provokes a sense of bewilderment and panic. It's easy to feel tossed about by economic and environmental storms. Institutions which have provided stability and continuity are failing, rules that once held firm have been violated and broken, and persons in leadership roles are falling into the traps of power-gone-awry. The externals of life to which we have looked for meaning—accomplishment, acquisition, and achievement—have let us down. The idols we have worshiped—relationships, success, knowledge, and substances—have failed us again and again. Having looked to these sources for meaning and security, we feel like victims in a world spinning out of control.

And so we hunger for real security in the midst of these troubling times. We long for meaning and purpose with a restlessness that can only be satisfied by a personal, vital love-relationship with Jesus Christ.

Even now, centuries after Jesus' physical presence calmed the waters for His disciples, His spiritual presence comes to His children. In that mysterious relationship between Creator and creature, Christ calls the believer to be still and to rest in Him. It is out of that inner connectedness with the Savior that direction and guidance and creativity flow. It is out of inner submission and the centeredness of being "in Christ" that the believer is able to live the abundant life.

At the beginning of this decade, I was hungry for inner stability and the ability to live from the inside instead of being at the mercy of others' choices and actions. Through my searching, I discovered a new way of praying. I came to see that it was possible to live a stable, victorious life, grounded and centered in the security of a relationship with Christ. I discovered that there was a way to avoid the trap of knee-jerk living and that the person who depends on God walks in balance. I found that my hunger was for God and that *nothing* else would fill that hunger. This life of creativity and productivity, of fulfillment and blessing, is possible *through prayer.*

It was during a period of searching in my young adulthood that I began to question the purpose and place of prayer. While I had prayed for as long as I could remember, I sensed myself being drawn to a deeper life. While I had known Christ as my Savior for many years, His Spirit beckoned me to a greater closeness and a more personal fellowship.

As I explored the types and ways of prayer, I encountered terms which were new and strange to me. These terms soon became more than mere words, but ways of going deeper in the life of prayer. These new practices ushered in a new era for me, pointing me toward inner strength and serenity instead of the external sources I had previously pursued. Whatever the cost, I wanted to live as a "contemplative" with the awareness of God's presence in all of life, sensing His activity in the common, everyday events.

When I attended my first contemplative weekend at the Church of the Saviour in Washington, D.C., I learned that *entering the silence* meant willfully choosing to draw apart from human voices for a period of time in order to listen for the voice of God. I learned

other new terms as well. I found that *the prayer of the heart* signi-
fied that inner fellowship between the heavenly Father and His
child. *Practicing the presence of God,* a condition of on-going communication between God and myself, came to be a discipline and
then, more and more, a way of life, so that every moment had the
possibility of encounter and conversation with God.

I have learned that God calls His children to the life of
prayer—out of love, He calls us to love. While I may have
thought that it was my idea to seek a deeper life of prayer, I now
know that my impulse was, in fact, a response. I was seeking Him
because He had first found me. Any inclination I had to His love
was the result of His having first loved me.

Meditation, for me, has come to be that act of placing my
attention on the love of God and allowing His love to do within
me whatever needs to be done at that time so that I can then let
His love flow through me to His creation and His children. *Creative silence is an exchange of love between God and the believer,
and that love then manifests itself in the world.*

Perhaps the contemplative life of practicing the presence of
Christ is calling to you. You may be interested in meditation
because of an inner hunger such as the one I had. Perhaps the
things you once trusted in no longer give you joy or peace. You
may have been tossed about by life's storms and are responding to
His invitation to come and draw from the well of Living Water.
You may simply be longing for the love of God.

In *Creative Silence,* I have shared my journey of prayer with the
hope that it will be a light to others who are inclined to this
journey. Each chapter describes a part of my journey and is intended to inspire fellow-pilgrims in the life of prayer.

The exercises given at the end of each chapter are patterns to
be used in nurturing the life of prayer. While a time of drawing
apart from the demands and responsibilities of life is desirable, the
discipline of a regular time of private worship each day cultivates
creative silence. These exercises can be used as one would use
finger exercises in learning how to play the piano. Using them is
like practicing the fundamentals of a sport. The discipline is necessary to encourage a contemplative lifestyle. It is possible to

"make retreat" each day by carving out a time to spend focused on God's presence.

As you follow the exercises in this book, you may find it helpful to keep a journal in which you record your pilgrimage in prayer. I personally think journal keeping is helpful in the whole process of spiritual growth.

As I wrote *Creative Silence*, there were people who appeared in my life at exactly the right time to give me encouragement. Some offered specific and practical help, and others shared their own experience. These encouragers were God's instruments of inspiration in my life, and I am deeply grateful for each one. My friends and guides along the pathway of prayer—Madeleine L'Engle, Howard Hovde, and Keith Hosey—have played vital roles of encouragement both in my spiritual development and in the writing of this book.

There were other teachers along the way—those I met in books; those who led me in retreats and seminars; those whom I led, women's groups and couple's groups, college students and individual seekers who were placed in my life as part of my journey. In the mysterious way of coincidence, as God broke through my circumstances over and over again, I found that I was teaching to others what I wanted to learn, and that was creative silence.

It was Floyd Thatcher whose able direction saw me from outline to acceptance of my manuscript for publication. Ruthi Seefeldt volunteered to put the original manuscript and my revisions on her word processor, and then she stayed firm in her belief in the manuscript for five years. My editor at Word, Beverly Phillips, has provided invaluable suggestions and careful attention to the details of *Creative Silence*.

My deep gratitude also goes to the Thursday morning Bible study group at Southland Baptist Church for their prayers of support and words of encouragement, and to many friends who have been a necessary part of the process.

May each of us live more fully in the light of Christ.

Jeanie Miley
San Angelo, Texas

C·h·a·p·t·e·r O·n·e

STEP INTO THE SUNSHINE . . .

*"Come to Me, all who are weary and heavy-laden, and
I will give you rest."*
—Matthew 11:28, NASB

*"Meditation is not so much a way to find God as it is a
way of resting in Him whom we have found, who loves
us, who is near to us, who comes to draw us to
Himself."*
—Thomas Merton

"I've followed the rules all my life, but it doesn't seem to matter. I feel locked in and trapped. I'm sick and tired of being sick and tired! Even my religion has become burdensome."

It was a tense declaration, punched into the cold, dreary afternoon. This lovely woman wore her self-punishment and defeat like a shroud as she and I trudged along our daily walk.

"I can turn anything good into something to feel bad about because I keep such a tight checklist of 'shoulds' and 'oughts.' Everything I do must be perfect. I manage to feel guilty about my family, my eating habits, and the way I use money and time! Nobody *makes* me feel guilty; I volunteer—*regularly!*"

Indeed, my uptight friend *had* kept all the rules, carefully checking off her lists of duties and obligations expected of a woman in her stage of life. What was missing? What was constricting the flow of joy and peace through her life? Why was she so tired and defeated?

We continued to walk, stepping up our pace as the tension mounted. I could feel the pain of my friend because I, too, know the anguish of keeping all the rules and missing out on the joy. I know how hard freedom is . . . and how easy slavery can be.

I hesitated, groping for a way to open up another alternative, to offer her a better possibility than the tense and tedious way of doing life which eventually leads to death of the spirit.

"Do you think God intends for you to live in such an uptight state?" I asked, fully aware even as the words left my mouth that my question would evoke more guilt.

"No, but . . ." she hesitated. "I almost feel as if I'm being punished."

"For what?" I demanded, incredulous that this model of right living could be guilty of anything.

"I don't know," she agonized. "Maybe I feel guilty more for what I haven't done than for what I have done. It's like there's something good and free inside me that's trying to get out, but I keep my brakes on so much that it can't break free!"

"Oh, *now* I understand," I cried. I knew well what she was talking about.

"There's a dream inside of me that wants to be born," she continued, "but it is dying because I'm so afraid."

"I know," I murmured, remembering. "It's like the lights have gone out!"

"Yes, that's exactly how it feels. All my life, I have felt that God wanted to do something through me, and I've tried to obey Him, most of the time. Now I wonder if I was doing all the wrong things. Did I hear Him wrong? I've tried so hard."

We walked on into the chilly dusk. I took a deep breath and gathered up my courage. "I have found a way to keep the lights on," I began. "Would you like to hear about it?"

* * *

Several years ago, for a number of most unholy reasons, I began to incorporate a time of prayer and meditation into my daily routine. Initially I sought the experience because I was hearing and reading about it from committed Christians whose lives were so attractive that I wanted to know what their secret was. Besides, *centering, focusing,* and *guided imagery* were being used in medicine, sports, business, the arts, and stress management. Maybe the secular world had found something the church had lost!

At the time, I was trying to make sense out of my life. I wanted peace and joy and all the other fruits of the Spirit. Selfishly, I wanted the deeper life so I could be more together; I wanted the power of Christ let loose in me . . . if it weren't too much trouble. Besides, I had heard, here and there, that I would be restless until I found rest in Christ, and so it seemed practical to me to get that situation settled.

Frankly, life was overwhelming me. The responsibilities of family life—balancing budgets, meeting the demands of work and community involvement—had become oppressive. My active lifestyle of good deeds and noble ventures had led me straightaway to burn-out. The tyranny of the "oughts" and "shoulds," the too much and too many of my cluttered days had depleted my reserves and revealed my need for a power greater than myself. The gaping emptiness I was experiencing was the logical, natural consequence of trying to live life on my own power. I had been on an outward journey, living in the fast lane of ministry and involvement, and it had depleted my energies. I yearned for release from the chains of fear, guilt, inferiority, and resentment so that I could love more fully. If the "leaping upon the mountains and skipping upon the hills" of the Song of Solomon was possible, I wanted to be in on it.

I wanted to make this inward journey, but I wasn't sure how to get started. Little did I realize that even in my mixed motives, God was calling me to an intimate, moment-by-moment fellowship with Him. Now I understand that the Master Designer used the circumstances of my life to get my attention. Through my discontent and dissatisfaction, He pushed me toward a deeper relationship. It was God Himself who started the conversation of prayer that is so much a part of my life today.

All along, God was in all the parts of my life, directing me toward the practice of His presence—a practice that would forge an inner stillness and release my bound creativity as He put me in touch with His intent and purpose for me. In the process, I discovered that Christian meditation is learning what He wants from me rather than giving Him my "To Do" list; meditation is the process by which He guides me into those areas where I can express my creativity, and then He gives me what I need to do His work. *The point of Christian meditation is to concentrate one's focus on the presence and power of Christ, to be filled with His love, and then to pass that love on into the world.*

* * *

The inner journey is what takes place as heart and mind work together. It is the work of Christ at the point of "the inner person," as opposed to the external keeping of laws or the changing of mere behavior. An inner journey frees the believer to live from the inside out rather than being tossed about by whatever comes from outside forces.

The roots of my inner journey reach deep into my past, and I see now that God was guiding me, calling me to prayer, and seeking me for friendship early in my childhood. Even as a child, I knew that God was everywhere and anywhere because my family practiced His presence. My father really believed that God was in charge of the universe and that He was an enormous, near reality. I will never forget the feeling of protection and security that swept over me as my father prayed. My mother, too, lived as though God were looking over her shoulder and might, at any moment, speak out loud. To me, that Presence was overwhelming and awesome.

As a child, I prayed by rote, out of habit or custom, or to please an adult. I prayed, too, out of fear, for my concept of God was shot through and through with His supreme might and power. As a teenager, I prayed when I needed forgiveness, fearing what He would do to me or ask from me, for I saw God as Judge and Jury. I also cried out for favors, and when they weren't delivered quickly, I decided prayer didn't "work."

In college, prayer was a frantic cry for help, a yearning for security in a rapidly-changing world, a reaching out into a reality I couldn't understand with a rational and intellectual point of view. I feared God's touching my emotions; one must, after all, stay in control.

During my college years, my early childhood trust was submerged by my intellectual pursuits, my growing social consciousness, and my efforts to live "in the real world." If I thought about the inner life of prayer at all, it was with only fleeting attention. Perhaps I thought I had "outgrown" that childlike dependency.

As I moved into adulthood, I sought footing in my new grownup responsibilities. My girlhood training had indeed formed a good base for adulthood, but the childlike practices of prayer were not adequate for the challenges of adult life, and I found myself moving from skepticism to an awareness that I either prayed amiss or without result. Since prayer didn't "work," then, I decided I would rely on my own efforts.

During the early seventies when there was much enthusiasm for prayer groups, I "tried" prayer again, but this approach didn't work for me either. Something in me resisted approaching God as a cosmic bellhop or a kindly old grandfather. Even then, I understood, though dimly, that God was not my servant. I wasn't sure, however, if I could be His.

I had moments when I "felt" God, but I had come to discount these times as emotional tricks. Once, immediately after our first child was born, I sensed a presence in my hospital room. That presence gave assurance and comfort in the midst of a fearful, stressful time. In my pseudo-sophisticated skepticism, however, I took years to recognize and acknowledge that "feeling" as God.

Later, as I began a journey of self-discovery, I had moments of intense awareness and sensitivity, of unusual perception or painful understanding which seemed to come from outside myself. Each of these experiences drew me closer to God; each prompted me to search for understanding in the Scriptures and in worship. Only now, in retrospect, have I identified those times of heightened awareness as God revealing Himself to me. Perhaps I would have recognized a whirlwind, but the still, small voice was harder to identify.

There was another time when I lay for hours in a labor room, waiting to go to surgery after a miscarriage. A serenity unlike any I had ever experienced enveloped me, bringing peace out of chaos and comfort out of despair. It took an older, wiser friend to pronounce it "grace" and "God" . . . and yet I still wondered.

I was familiar, too, with parts of my life that had come together in amazing ways that defied mere coincidence. Such moments of harmonious arrangement stood out as evidence of what I supposed to be supernatural activity. It was easy, because of the faith of my father and mother, to believe in the *idea* of supernatural activity in the common, everyday events of life, but it was hard for me to assert that God had done this or that or to claim that "God told me" something.

When I began to seek for something more, I wasn't really sure what that would be. *Was* it the true meaning and experience of prayer I was looking for, or did I need to know more facts about the life and teachings of Christ? I had learned more principles for improving interpersonal relationships than I was putting into practice, and I had been given valuable, helpful tools for self-understanding and self-actualization. So, why was I still restless?

Slowly, almost imperceptibly, I began to understand that my search was, after all, a search for God, and I knew that my heart would indeed not rest until I had found myself in intimacy with the Father. Was prayer the missing link, the key to abundant life? I wondered.

As I look back with wiser eyes, I see that one of the most significant guideposts along the way of my journey to a more fulfilling prayer life was a book entitled *With Open Hands* by Henri Nouwen.

One restless night, with questions about prayer assaulting my mind, I leafed through this slim volume which is now worn and marked. I *wanted* to believe that prayer was worth the time and trouble, that it was more than securing favors or groveling for forgiveness.

Hungrily, I read until I came to the page which answered my questioning.

Deep silence leads us to suspect that, in the first place, prayer is acceptance. A man who prays is a man standing with his hands open to the world. He knows that God will show himself in the nature which surrounds him, in the people he meets, in the situations he runs into. He trusts that the world holds God's secret within it, and he expects that secret to be shown to him. Prayer creates that openness where God can give himself to man. Indeed, God wants to give himself; he wants to surrender himself to the man he has created, he even begs to be admitted into the human heart.[1]

Reverently, I wrote the date, June 12, 1977, on page 56. I had an answer. There in the darkness of the night, I opened my hands and my heart to God in prayer and began to accept His new agenda for the next stage of life.

Later, when I questioned my husband about the book, neither of us knew how it had gotten into our library.

Within days, a friend casually used the phrase "abiding in Christ," and I was propelled along another avenue. The next week, I found Andrew Murray's *Abide in Christ*, and it became my inspiration for the next portion of my journey. Gently, methodically, I was being led by some force that seemed to come from without and within at the same time. As I became ready, the teacher appeared. The search for silence as a way to God was becoming real at last.

The questions that began to emerge were "How do I pray without ceasing?" and "How do I practice the presence of God?" The answers would come in time, but one thing I knew for sure: If prayer was the key to triumphant living and the way to release the energy and power of God, I wanted it! I wanted the joy of the presence of God as an ongoing reality. How to maintain that presence was the question that dominated my thoughts when my husband and I decided to attend a silent retreat at the Church of the Saviour in Washington, D.C.

Martus and I left our year-old church and three young daughters in San Angelo, Texas, to participate in a four-day orientation and an eight-day workshop at Wellspring Retreat Center of this unusual church begun by Gordon Cosby. We were captivated by what we had read of their emphasis on the balance between the inner journey of prayer and the outer journey of ministry. And we wanted to learn more about individual giftedness and call being the outgrowth of the inner life of prayer, Bible study, and personal accountability.

I could hardly wait for the silent part of the experiences. My friends had teased me unmercifully. They were certain I could never stay quiet for the two-and-one-half day experience, but there was no doubt in my mind that I could do it. Somehow, meeting God in the silence seemed to be just what I needed to turn life's next corner.

*   *   *

Thunder clapped a loud amen to the silent retreat as I ran quickly through the rain to the retreat center. I paused on the wide, covered porch, memorizing the misty scene of this Maryland countryside, the smell of the rain and the dancing sounds it made on the roof.

The rain had nurtured me through the days and nights of silence like a healing balm. I had been dry and weary, arriving from the parched, West Texas desert to participate in a new pilgrimage. I had come to Wellspring to discover more ways of knowing God, and for two and one-half days, I had stumbled around, trying to calm my restlessness enough to be still and know God.

I was awkward in the newness of silence. In the long, hushed days I had moved from writing in my journal to reading. Trying to meditate, I moved back and forth from the bed to the chair in my small, cell-like room in the Lodge of the Carpenter. When the rain paused, I would try the outdoors, hoping to "find" God in the wooded paths or along the slender stream. My discomfort with this new discipline accelerated at meal times. We strangers gathered to eat together, clumsily "asking" for the salt to be passed with eye and hand signals. Self-consciousness betrayed our inner nervousness. I was more conscious of external cues than I was of the voice of God within me.

Even the terminology of the retreat leaders had put me off a bit. "Entering the silence," "centering in," and "seeking God's presence" seemed so other-worldly. I was a hesitant risker, and yet I knew my being there was part of a plan. My instincts told me that this journey inward, as they called it, was the next part of my pilgrimage.

Now, as we gathered for our reporting time, I was really nervous. Only moments before, I had sat down in my tiny room for one more attempt to experience the presence of Christ. Suddenly, and with no effort on my part, a quietness that was filled with meaning I didn't understand crept into the room.

Was this "encounter," I wondered. Is this what I'd been striving for? The fleeting impression of the Presence stayed with me as I gathered up my journal and made my way along the gravel path to the Lodge.

Now that it was time to "come out of the silence" and report to each other, the noises of our gathering offended my ears. I wanted to linger in quietness a little longer, and so I avoided all eye contact, feeling strangely shy back in the sounds of community.

A raindrop shot down my back, sending a shiver over my body. Or was it discomfort I was feeling, knowing that within moments I would have to report on my days of silence and meditation? I wasn't sure my effort measured up; I clutched my journal and scurried inside.

A bearded fellow lay spongelike on the floor. I supposed he was a yogi. Other retreat participants wrote in their journals while some sat quietly, gazing into the distance. Were they feeling as awkward as I? Had the silence been stranger or friend? Would my brief, fleeting awareness of the living Christ, my faltering efforts to center on Him hold up with their glittering success stories? Had anyone really had a mountaintop experience?

Warmed by a cozy fire, one after another reported on "finding" God in the quietness. They read from journals and spoke with assurance about experiencing the presence of God as they walked in the woods and bathed in the streams.

My paltry efforts to be still and know God would have been acceptable, but I held back. These stories evoked memories of retreat testimonies of emotional highs which dissolved in the routine of daily life. The glorious experiences always seemed far removed from my efforts to survive the conflicts and perils of life.

I needed, desperately, then and now, for someone to admit honestly and forthrightly that it wasn't all victorious.

I listened, sometimes believing, but more often skeptical. I held back my own experience, for the cultivation of my inner life was too new, too fragile to parade before these strangers. Besides, I couldn't risk losing control or appearing foolish. Little did I know that the very restraints I had placed on myself would become the growing edge in my meditation; I had no idea that part of God's purpose in calling me to meditation was to unlock my real self. He wanted to peel back the layers of limitation and error to reveal the secret of whom He had called me to be.

"I didn't know, when we started, about this God-talking-to-you business," one of the participants blurted out.

The terribly serious mood was shattered, and we all turned to scrutinize this skeptic who had halted the momentum of success stories with her simple, frank confession.

I looked at her with relief and amusement. Her straightforward assertion had brought us down from the clouds to the reality of walking the tightrope of faith in the common, ordinary routine of life.

This endearing disturber peered at us over the thick glasses she wore low on her nose. "Nothing happened to me until right at the end," she declared. "I didn't want to come back over here and report that I hadn't seen or heard God."

At last! Someone had voiced my concern. Somebody else was experiencing the same frustration I was experiencing on my spiritual pilgrimage—the frustration of yearning and seeking and stumbling around. This honest soul had walked in my shoes. I listened intently as she continued.

"I finally sat down just a few minutes ago, and said, 'Well, *are* you there, God?'"

Bessie's bluntness blew away our pretenses at holiness and opened us up to be who we really were, fellow-strugglers on a new and unfamiliar journey. We laughed together, relieved from the need to be something we were not. We were relaxed and open once again because someone had dared to reveal her doubts.

"And what did God say, Bessie?" asked our retreat leader gently.

Bessie paused to collect herself, and a warm silence nestled among us.

"He said, 'I'm right here, Bessie!'" she replied.

We wept . . . because He was there and because we understood.

EXERCISE

This inner life of prayer need not be left to chance. For those who want to cultivate a sense of God's presence, there are specific tasks which will make this possible. There are things you can do which will develop your awareness and sensitivity to God's presence. By disciplining your mind, you can make retreat throughout the day. These exercises, then, provide a way to discover that presence of God within you, and then out of the silence, your own creativity will awaken and express itself.

Find a quiet place where you know you will not be disturbed. Returning to the same place at the same time each day will be beneficial. It is helpful to practice the meditation twice a day; the important thing is to be consistent. God does indeed meet us when we turn to Him.

Choose a posture that is comfortable for you. You may prefer sitting in a straight-back chair, with legs uncrossed, hands resting quietly in your lap with palms turned upward in a gesture of openness and trust. You may want to kneel.

A good place to begin is with the Scriptures. Read Psalm 16, 23, or 100 slowly, focusing on each verse. Soon, however, close your eyes and breathe deeply, allowing your body to relax. Commit this time to God, asking His Spirit to be your guide.

Picture Christ sitting beside you. Hear Him say, "I am with you always," or "My peace I give to you."

Another method of focusing on the Presence is to pray the Jesus Prayer several times. It is simply: "Lord Jesus Christ, Son of the living God, have mercy on me, a sinner." This is not intended to be a chant; it is simply a way to rivet your attention on Christ.

Remain silent and still for at least ten minutes—when your mind wanders, don't fight the distracting thought or feel guilty. Calmly, gently, bring your mind back to the awareness of God's presence. Tell that nagging thought, as you would an interrupting child, that you will see to it as soon as you have finished praying.

Do not judge or evaluate this time. You are drawing apart as an act of obedience. Receive whatever is there in the silence, trusting God to give you exactly what He desires for this time.

As you return more gently and quietly to your daily routine, be aware that you are always in the presence of God.

Throughout the day, take sixty seconds to focus your awareness on God's presence within you.

LET'S GET PRACTICAL

"Go in by the narrow gate.
For the wide gate has a broad road which leads to disaster
and there are many people going that way.
The narrow gate and the hard road lead out into life
and only a few are finding it."
Matthew 7:13–14, PHILLIPS

"It is impossible to learn how to meditate from a book.
We learn to meditate by meditating."
—Richard Foster

"We do not want to be beginners.
But let us be convinced of the fact that
we will never be anything else but beginning all our life."
—Thomas Merton

"It must be nice to go off to a quiet place for a spiritual retreat," my friend's voice crackled over the telephone against a background buzz of noisy children.

"But what I'd like to know is how I can have this Presence you talk about right here in this house!"

It was a challenge, sputtered across hundreds of miles to jolt me out of my clouds of ideas and into the reality of communicating practical suggestions for maintaining an inner stillness in a noisy, chaotic world. Somehow, I had to translate my experiences in practicing the presence of God into practical aid!

What *does* meditation offer that is good enough to entice a busy homemaker to get up early or to stay up late in order to spend moments in silent communion with the Unseen? How does meeting God in silence restore, renew, and release the creative spark of the abundant life?

My friend's challenge caused me to recognize that not everyone would respond to the particular methods I had used and sent me searching for other tools of the inner life.

I wanted to de-mystify the experience of meditation, but I didn't want to cheapen the mystery. It was important to me to show that this kind of fellowship with Christ was not for an esoteric few, but for every believer. I wanted to show others how the very things and events of everyday life can lead to a deeper friendship with Christ.

What would I tell my friend, then, about getting started? What methods or tools would I pass along to enhance the possibility of this encounter?

I discovered that some basic guidelines seem to help the process, and while they may seem simple or simplistic, they do not necessarily come easily.

First of all, it is important to establish a routine and find a place which will be consistently private and quiet. I soon learned that it became easier for me to move into my prayers when I returned each day to the same familiar place. With practice, the reserved time seemed to wait for me. After a while, I no longer debated about whether I would or wouldn't withdraw for prayer. My time of drawing away came as naturally as mealtime.

It is also helpful to use breathing and relaxation techniques. I would recommend practicing exercises which sharpen awareness and increase concentration, such as those at the end of each chapter in this book.

It is important to train your mind and senses, too. Learn to contemplate by closely observing a portion of God's creation. Make a habit of becoming very still throughout the day, listening and asking, "What is God trying to say to me right now?" Practice pondering objects of nature to develop your ability to focus and stay centered. "Focusing" and "centering," or concentrating, are skills that can be developed as you practice paying attention to something. As you discipline your mind, using Scripture and prayer as your focus, you will grow in your ability to stay centered in an attitude of prayer. More and more, you will sense God's presence working within you, and you will not so easily be thrown off course by external events.

Finally, it is important to clear your mind of worries and frustrations. Imagine yourself putting a problem "on the back burner" or leaving it outside the door in a brown paper bag or "putting brackets" on a particular situation for a stated period of time. The purpose of meditation is to encounter God, not to solve problems, enjoy fantasies, or daydream.

In the early stages of attempting to meditate, I had to resort to setting a clock at intervals throughout the day to remind me to turn my attention to God and His presence with me. I worked hard at setting aside the same time each morning and evening to turn my heart toward Him, enclosing the day in His presence. But I also began to incorporate the attitude of prayer throughout all the activities and conversations of the day.

As I mentioned earlier, praying the Jesus Prayer, "Lord Jesus Christ, Son of the living God, have mercy on me, a sinner," is another way of reminding myself that I am in the presence of God. Read John 17 to discover Christ's prayer for you, as He prayed for His disciples. He prayed that His heavenly Father would keep you in His presence, give you joy, keep you from the evil one, and sanctify you (set you apart). Christ's purpose for each of us is that we should know Christ with an intimate familiarity and not just mere facts.

Using Scripture creatively can bring revelation and insight. Try reading through a favorite Psalm, for example, until you come to a phrase or verse which speaks to you. Pause and let its teachings sink deeply into your awareness. What is its truth for you today?

In a similar vein, try reading a scene from one of the Gospels and then picture yourself in an imagined encounter with Christ. Imagine the sights, sounds, and smells of the scenes in Jesus' life. How did it feel when Jesus healed you? Were you in the crowd when the woman of ill-repute washed Jesus' feet with expensive perfume? Or were you the woman at the well? Can you imagine how the disciples felt as they witnessed the water turned into wine? Perhaps you relate to Nicodemus or the man who was brought on a pallet to Jesus. What would you like for Jesus to do or be for you this day?

Relational Bible studies, which will help you with this discipline, are given in Karl Olson's book, Come to the Party.[2] These Bible studies will involve you in the personal relationships found in Scripture, and will enable you to relate the truths you find to your own relationships. Lloyd John Ogilvie is another author who makes Scripture come alive in his Bible expositions—I especially like Life Without Limits, Drumbeat of Love, and Let God Love You. The important challenge is to live the Scriptures by internalizing them.

As you use your imagination to taste and feel and see the encounters of Christ with the men and women of His day, you will identify with them and their responses to Him. Then, as you soak yourself in the stories, you will find yourself "praying the Scriptures," and this will lead you into Truth. (Praying the Scriptures is an ancient way of meditation which opens the way for deep communion with God. Choose one of the Psalms and begin to read it slowly and carefully. When a phrase or a verse catches your attention, pause to ponder its meaning, turning it over and over in your mind. Repeat the phrase, re-read the passage that has "chosen" you, and it will teach you. As you immerse your mind in the words of the Psalms, your mind will be transformed.)

One of the things I have learned about the spiritual life is that it is necessary to give up the notion that you and I can be in control or that we will become experts. God is in control, and part of the process involves letting Him lead us into growth. That creates a feeling of newness, which means we will always feel like we are just beginning the journey.

There are no tricks, shortcuts, or special gimmicks in the spiritual life. It is up to us to put ourselves in the position to receive God's gift of prayer; once we have done that, the work of prayer is God's responsibility. The inner work of prayer—that teaching, healing, guiding, and restoring process that takes place when we draw near—is God's work in us, transforming our minds and hearts. Therefore, we must relax and allow Him to do His work. He will not expect maturity of us which we haven't attained; but once we have attained it, he will expect us to act accordingly.

The desire to know God is a gift of grace, and our turning toward Him pleases Him. It is important to accept the time of meditation as God's gift, guarding it carefully. Through an act of your will, claim the courage to begin and to continue your prayer time, even when nothing is happening. Do not look frantically from side to side, trying to see God at work. Instead, do what is required of you each day, and He will act. Accept even His silence as part of His work of grace.

God speaks through His world and through other people. He meets us in the theater or in a book, in a child's question or in a perplexing problem. His love extends all around, so don't fret about how He will speak to you or if He will; simply develop an attitude of watchfulness as you go about your daily activities.

In recent years, I have learned to pay closer attention to images and pictures that pass, seemingly unbidden, through my mind. I have begun writing these down, along with my dreams. Sometimes they are inconsequential, but at times, God speaks through the images.

Several years ago, while on vacation in Lake City, Colorado, I was working through some significant, but typical, mid-life questions. One evening, as I finished my daily walk, my eyes happened to move to an upstairs window in one of the old brick buildings. For some reason, the window, open to the cool breeze, became a symbol for my next year's pilgrimage into new experiences.

Coincidence? Perhaps. But, then again, the Unseen One speaks in mysterious ways. I have learned to see that the turn of my thoughts toward God is the result of His movement toward me. The appearance of something pleasant will provoke a spontaneous prayer of thanks; the eruption of a problem will send me immediately to the Source of strength. A sudden insight will remind me that I'm on Holy Ground, in the presence of the Almighty. And the process of meditation prepares my willful heart to receive the practical and specific aid of the Holy Spirit.

Those who have practiced the presence of God have learned certain helps along the way which you may want to use.

First, stay in community with other believers who can fan the flame of Christ's life in you. If possible, find someone who can act as a spiritual director or sponsor for you. This must be a person who has been on the journey of spiritual growth longer than you have—someone who can guide you and direct you in your pilgrimage, always pointing you beyond himself or herself to the Source.

You may also want to try meditating as you walk or jog. I've found that when I read a thought from one of the great devotional writers just before I leave the house, it often leads me to new discoveries about the Christ-life as I walk my familiar trail. Although my body may be on autopilot, my mind will be busy; so I might as well give it useful, positive thoughts to contemplate! Using that time to memorize Scripture is another way to keep the mind focused and ready for an encounter with God.

When I first began to listen for the still, small Voice, I was appalled to discover instead a committee of voices, demands, cues, and arguments going on in my head. No wonder I was often tired and confused! I had a habit of trying to please everyone else, often in the name of "service." My dependency on others' approval had become an addiction. Now God was calling me out of all that anguish, beckoning me toward home.

As I attempted to be still and know God, I wiggled and twitched like a small child. I found it nerve-racking to sit still for small periods of time. Sleepiness plagued me, and the more I fought it, the heavier my eyelids became. I had read about a monk, Brother Lawrence, who had learned to practice the presence of God as he went about his work in a monastery kitchen long ago. His pattern of bringing worship to work and making the most mundane task a time of "meeting God" appealed to me. I thought I would try that, and my plan was to get up very early to get my mind focused on God's presence, to offer my day to Him, and to ask Him for His guidance throughout my chores and activities.

Schedules disrupted by my young children discouraged me as I attempted to set a routine time for my encounter with God. As surely as I would get up early to practice the presence of God, my toddler would choose to welcome the day with me! If I tried to carve out a moment's privacy in the nighttime hours, one or more of my three children would be sick, and I would be up all night. Over and over, I began again and again.

There were days when I struggled to make myself go through the discipline of quietness; other days I didn't even try. There were periods of despair when I would cry out for a cloud or a pillar of fire to give me direction in a dark period. I wanted to abandon the journey because it seemed so hard, and when I heard Keith Hosey, my friend and gifted teacher, say, "The way to awareness of God's presence is too steep and too difficult for those who are not called to that journey by God," I considered turning in my ticket for an easier pilgrimage. I couldn't leave for long, however; God pursued me through the ups and downs of life, repeatedly bringing me back to the realization that my life is unmanageable without Him.

I was tempted to give up. My failures at consistency nearly defeated me. Eventually, I came to a point where I recognized that I was going to have to trust God to *keep* me abiding in His presence.

"OK, God," I said one day, "I've made a decision to turn my life over to you. If I change my mind, I'll let you know. Meanwhile, I'm going to stick it out, no matter how hard it gets, and I need for you to help me!"

I dug in my heels, and I thought I heard God chuckle. He knew what He was doing all along.

As I ventured on, there were brief periods of satisfaction where I would feel God was honoring my journey. At other times, I didn't know if my efforts were working, but I kept on plodding along. Over and over, I surrendered and abandoned myself to God, always seeking evidence of His presence in my life.

Repeatedly, I affirmed God's presence, His sovereignty, and my desire to abandon myself to Him in complete trust. I would claim His power as I began an endeavor. The words and prayers of surrender were familiar in my mouth, and I confessed a desire for the words to mold and reflect my will. I hoped that the disciplined periods of prayer that were devoid of feeling would somehow, someday pay off—that the feelings would catch up with my affirmations.

If the truth in the parable of the seed could be trusted—if, indeed, God Himself could be trusted—then I had to keep doing my part and trust that God would bring to harvest what He wanted harvested. I had to accept the reality that, in the life of prayer, I might always *feel* like a beginner.

Developing a friendship with Christ is not an easy journey, and one who starts on the journey should count the cost ahead of time (Luke 14:28–29). Once you begin, however, God will provide you the fortitude to continue and the courage to accept the beams of light—those moments when God breaks through the fog with evidence of His presence—as they come. He will teach you to relax in the everlasting arms of the Savior.

*   *   *

The day was overcast when I set out for the Quiet House at the HEB Foundation Camp near Leakey, Texas, but I felt protected and empowered. I drove toward the Texas Hill Country with the growing conviction that God was preparing the way, even as I was traveling. Somehow at a deeper, unacknowledged level, I had known that someday I would go away to find silence in this special place created for seekers of intimacy with God.

To leave responsibility for three days of private retreat was a luxury alien to me. Friends who did not understand thought my need for solitude absurd; others looked at me with disbelief. The scattered few who knew me well sent me away with blessings and encouragement. I needed their affirmation, for I was unaccustomed to doing anything that might not meet the approval of others.

The Quiet House, like a mini cathedral, has a wonderful, sunlit loft. Childlike, I headed for it soon after I arrived at the camp. Once I had made my way to the loft's sunny heights, the awareness of what had brought me to this place and point in time washed over me with stunning clarity.

I must come away to the quiet in order to remember who I am! I thought . . . or was it spoken to me? That centering awareness also included the quiet knowledge of *whose* I am. My faltering efforts at knowing God had brought me to a new level of encounter: now I was to begin learning how to worship in that inner quietness in the busy arena of everyday life.

Suddenly, I recognized the process for what it was. The climbing and searching, the plodding and waiting had finally brought me to the point of recognition. I sat, quiet and still in the sunshine, so keenly aware of the presence of God that I didn't want to move or break the holiness of the moment. I had come home at last. My search had led me to find that God truly was within me.

I laughed to myself as I looked back over the past years, recognizing the order of my journey. I had learned that my temperament is such that people-pleasing is a constant temptation for me and threatens my peace of mind, the exercise of my gifts, and my obedience to God. How appropriate for God's work to touch the area of my deep need and pain! How freeing it was to sense His liberating touch in my most difficult area of bondage! How good it was to come home to myself and to God in a new way, to come to my senses and to a new kind of inner harmony. The silence stilled the committee of voices in my head so that I could, at last, hear the still, small voice. I was beginning to learn how it *felt* for God to speak in the silence to reassure me that I am His child, created by His design to fulfill His purposes.

After a night's rest, I settled into a routine of Bible reading and prayer, writing in my journal, and resting. As I began to relax and listen, I became aware, first of all, of the messages going on in my head. Later, I began to sense God's presence, and His presence brought peace.

Back at home, I learned that I could take small moments throughout the day to turn my attention to God's presence by thanking Him for specific gifts, by asking for His help, by savoring some beauty in nature or in someone's face. Practicing the presence of God can take place in the midst of the marketplace, and whenever I think to turn my attention to God in the midst of that busyness, I know that it is because His spirit has tapped me on the shoulder.

In the silence I find my worth as a child of God, a unique creature infinitely loved and sustained by the Source of Life. As the Spirit of God guides and instructs in the quietness, I am loved by the One who made me, and that primary intimacy sets my other intimacies and relationships in a proper perspective.

Fellowship with the living Christ gives me new eyes to see the world more nearly as it is instead of viewing it through the distortion of my own experience or need-level. Perhaps, this keener insight is the wisdom to see myself and others with the mind of Christ. The joys are deeper; the participation in the suffering of the world is greater because of the awareness of the presence of the Lamb of God.

Throughout the challenges of life, I participate in my share of misunderstandings and broken relationships. When these incidents erupt, my natural response is to focus in on what I want, what I am feeling, how I have been hurt or how someone else has taken advantage of me. I can work up a good case of self-pity or cast myself as the innocent victim; I know these roles well.

However, if I am practicing my daily surrender, I can move much more quickly into seeing the situation through the eyes of reconciliation—my self-absorbed myopia is repaired, and I can more quickly see the whole picture rather than my narrow corner of the world. As I give God permission to work, healing power is released and transformation evolves.

Out of the silence comes focused energy. Creativity is released and ideas come together with amazing clarity if I have taken the time to center on the Giver of life. Instead of jumping from one task to another, I stay in the mainstream of what is important. And I waste fewer steps when I have taken time to wait for God's direction. I have tested what Martin Luther said about needing more time for prayer as more demands were facing him by carving out special moments of prayer during especially busy times. It is true. I discovered that the discipline of focusing in *before the fact* activates my awareness that it truly is God who goes behind and before, making the crooked straight and the road level.

Through the years since I first began to meditate, I have meandered up and down different paths as I've explored various philosophies and techniques. My curiosity and research have taken me down a few blind alleys. I have found my way and then lost it again. I have been both elated and discouraged. I have felt and known the presence of God in might and power only to question, later, if it really was God.

In Luke 15, we read that when the Prodigal Son left his father's house and the fellowship he had there, he drifted into waste and wanton living. The "far country" for him was a state of ruin and humiliation, separated from home and family by his own choices. I haven't gone into the particular "far country" that the Prodigal Son explored, but I've muddled and strayed my way in and out of fellowship with God and with His people, sometimes by carelessness and neglect, and at other times by open rebellion to the disciplines of freedom.

I haven't made the choice to live in union once, but many times, and there is still struggle at each deciding point. I still confront fear and doubt; I confront a laziness that tempts me to take the path of least resistance, the road too often traveled to mediocrity and surface living.

When I do stray from the higher call, a divine discontent usually sets in. I become confused and estranged from God and others, and my fear mounts to gargantuan levels. The Correcting Spirit pursues me even as He allows me to turn aside.

However, when I have made the first step back toward the Father's house, He has met me every time, lavishing love and grace and mercy, tenderly tending my self-inflicted wounds, and, best of all, throwing a party to welcome me back into fellowship. The party comes in the form of a renewed sense of purpose and direction, a restored relationship, or a breakthrough of insight. Regardless of the way God meets me, I have the feeling of coming home, of coming to my senses.

The invitation to creative living is an open one, and what is offered is a banquet. Coming home to the party that the Father has planned is part of the purpose of meditation. He offers the invitation freely and expectantly and waits eagerly for our response.

It is scary to take another's word that the journey is worth the effort, but it is the Lord of the Universe who is offering the invitation, not His human instruments. And He can, indeed, be trusted.

> Entrance into prayer is an act of faith. Praying is simply believing that we are in the mystery of God, that we are encompassed by that mystery, that we are really plugged into and immersed into it—'in Him we live and move and have our being' (Acts 17:28)—that the mystery of God in its fullness is both inside and outside, within and without, like the air which surrounds us and penetrates into the tiniest hollows of our lungs.[3]

It is possible to live "in the envelope of God's grace" in the twentieth century. It is possible because God is continually broadcasting His love to His creation. Meditation, simply, makes it possible to tune in to the message and the Messenger.

Perhaps you would like to respond to His invitation.

> "Ho! Every one who thirsts, come to the waters" (Isaiah 55:1, NASB).

> ". . . Whoever drinks of the water that I shall give him shall never thirst; but the water that I shall give him shall become in him a well of water springing up to eternal life" (John 4:14, NASB).

> ". . . I am the bread of life; he who comes to Me shall not hunger, and he who believes in Me shall never thirst" (John 6:35, NASB).

EXERCISE

If you are reading this book, chances are that you, too, are being called to the deeper life of prayer. You, too, are likely responding to the Love of the Father, the invitation to the party.

To prepare yourself for this time of encounter, follow the same relaxation suggestions given at the end of Chapter 1.

In your meditation time, become aware of your concept of God. How do you experience Him? With fear and dread, or gladness and trust? With guilt or with eagerness?

To become focused on God's involvement with you and care for you, read Psalm 46.

Picture Christ actually living, dwelling, abiding in you.

Repeat "The Father is very fond of me," and picture His taking delight in you.

How does His joy in you feel?

How does it feel to know that God longs to give Himself to you in loving power?

How does it feel to know that Christ lives *in* you?

Listen for the Word of God to you this day. When you think He may be speaking to you, write down the dialogue.

Write your prayers in a journal.

Keep a record of your thoughts, your unfolding.

Write down what you think God may be praying to you. You may be surprised!

JOY—THAT INFALLIBLE SIGN

"Our obedience and surrender to God
are in large part our obedience and surrender to our gifts.
This is the message wrapped up in the parable
of the talents.
Our gifts are on loan. We are responsible
for spending them in the world, and we will be
held accountable."
—Elizabeth O'Connor

"I will set you over much; enter into the joy
of your master."
—Matthew 25:21-23, RSV

"Joy is the most infallible sign of the presence of God."
—Teilhard de Chardin

"Everyone is gifted," the small, dark woman declared to a banquet-room filled with Junior League ladies. Ann McGee-Cooper had totally captured the attention of the participants in the Area V Seminar.

"Everyone is creative," she continued. "If you say you're not, you're not. But, if you agree that you are and are willing to let yourself go in finding and expressing your creativity, it is like tapping into the resources of an unlimited bank account! You must be *willing* to be creative."

I'm not sure when I began to notice it, but after several months of practicing the presence of God, I began to experience all sorts of creative urges. It was as if the living Christ within me was seeking self-expression through me. This surge of life sprung up in new insights and energy. I seemed tuned in to a different level of awareness and could pull things together—writing, teaching, living—with some sort of new power. Even when I didn't know what to call it, the creative force of God was working its way out into acts of love. God was expressing a part of Himself through my uniqueness and my creativity even before I knew what was happening.

As that creativity began to be freed in expression, I sensed the joy of God's presence as never before, and I began to see the joy of others who were willing to be His instruments in expressing their creativity. I noticed a zest and a vigor in the people who let God use them for His purposes. I began to see creativity and joy as two powerful forces, connected in a way I'd never imagined.

Ann's message was exactly the encouragement I needed for the next part of my journey. I was hearing from the secular world what I had discovered in the life of meditation. When I am centered in Christ, my work and my creativity are like prayer, flowing spontaneously through me. Somehow, Ann's speech gave me courage to put together and express what I had come to believe so deeply about creativity and prayer. I had discovered that meditation releases creativity and that creativity, once expressed, has everything to do with joyful living.

Creativity is not confined only to the intuitive and imaginative or to the arts, but it can also be expressed in logical, segmented, linear thinking and activities. New ways of thinking about creativity and giftedness are revolutionizing education; *Drawing on the Right Side of the Brain,* by Betty Edwards, details the blending of right- and left-brain creativity. There are those who are gifted in logical, straight-line thinking and others who draw more on their intuitive strengths. But true creativity uses both sides of the brain. Or stated another way, whole-brain thinking enhances creativity.

Moving back and forth between the theoretical and the practical, the thinking and doing, leads to creative living; likewise, the process of meditation feeds the creative process. Each time my husband

and I lead a BiPolar Relationship Seminar (a process which identifies the value and function of differing strengths), we discover that when individual wholeness is expressed as both independence and dependence, theoretical and practical polarities are strengthened and used.

Basic to the ministry of the Church of the Saviour is the belief and practice that every Christian is called by God and called to use his gifts in ministry. As part of our workshop at the Church of the Saviour, we had been asked to define our call, or to make our own mission statement. Using some background experience and taking a look at personal desires and talents, we were led through a thorough group process of discovery and assessment, *which had been preceded by the silent days of prayer.*

With fear and trembling, I tentatively expressed that I believed I had been called to the ministry of reconciliation through teaching and writing. While it scared me to death to commit myself to those words, there was also an accompanying sense of excitement and adventure. I wondered what God would have for me if I launched out of my safe place to "do my call," to express my own giftedness in ministry.

Personally, I had experienced that as I grew in my openness and receptivity to God, I had begun to find my place. I had discovered my giftedness and was struggling to relax enough to claim it and let it flow! I had even started, though tentatively, to define and implement what I believed was God's call, and as I had lived into that call, I began to see how God had been preparing me for that call all of my life through circumstances I hadn't even recognized. I began to see that I had the gifts to respond to that call; indeed, God had opened opportunities for training and skill-building in the most unusual and unpredictable ways and places. He had affirmed my call through "successes" and through open doors. The response of others to my work was gratifying and encouraging.

Furthermore, I had that "Eureka" feeling when I was doing my call. My mind could come up with dozens of more ideas for the exercise of the call. It felt natural and free, spontaneous, fun, and "right." All I needed was the courage to accept the freedom to do the work He had called me to.

We ask to know the will of God without guessing that his will is written into our very beings. We perceive that will when we discern our gifts.[4]

As I have explored both creativity and prayer, it has become clear that the two processes go hand in hand. As Madeleine L'Engle says in *Walking on Water*, "The disciplines of the creative process and Christian contemplation are almost identical. One is the outgrowth of the other, and each feeds and nourishes the other." My prayer and my life work—that effort, whether paid or volunteer, which gives meaning to my life, which excites me, and which I feel is important to the kingdom of God—flow as I center my will in God. My prayer and my work are both responses to Love and gifts to love.

For several years I taught a Self-Assessment and Self-Management course originated by Alena Morris, the director of the Individual Development Center in Seattle, Washington. As I saw people claim their giftedness through this course, I became more and more convinced that discovering and doing what one is created to do is one of the most important learning tasks of life. I soon saw that expressing personal giftedness is an antidote for depression.

When my energies and attention are focused on doing what I love and enjoy, I look forward to getting up in the morning and going about my work. When I feel that what I contribute is meaningful to someone else and that it is needed, I feel that sense of joy and purpose that keeps my attention turned to something other than my own self-centeredness.

Sometimes I try to squirm out of the responsibility for using my gifts by discounting them ("I really don't think anyone cares") or by wasting my energy fearing that I'll fail. However, when I push through the pain of fear and the resistance to exercising my call with my gifts, God *rushes* to honor my overcoming with a new surge of refreshed energy and creativity—a reminder that He never calls us to something without providing for the call and that, in the midst of cooperating with Him to accomplish His dream, joy begins to grow.

We who call ourselves Christian are under a divine imperative. We are responsible for discovering, developing, and using our talents. We will be held accountable for how we have used or squandered our gifts.

*   *   *

Sandra Hulse, my artist friend, beamed her probing eye deep into my soul one day over lunch. I was making excuses for not writing because it was "so hard."

"I'd hate to have to stand before God on Judgment Day and tell Him I hadn't been responsible for the gift he gave me!" she said.

Her pronouncement seemed a little strong over taco salad, and yet she pushed me into claiming responsibility. Indeed, I knew I had no joy when I quelled God's purpose or his call. The more I sat on my gifts, the more miserable I was, and the more misery I gave my loved ones and friends.

I began venturing out with some writing projects I had wanted to do, but had been too scared to attempt. As I began to see my teaching, both within our church and in small growth groups, as part of my mission and call instead of merely filling a slot, my teaching took on a new, exciting dimension. With a new way of perceiving my tasks, I lost my fear of speaking in front of a group and began to enjoy communicating in retreats and workshops. My skills as a homemaker, wife, and mother took on new meaning as I saw them as an important part of my reason for being.

Using one's gifts is not an ego trip, but a *service*, and each of us is a servant of Jesus Christ, called to do His work, to serve His creation. If I cooperate with Him, I will be moved and changed and blessed; if I say no to what I have been called to, I give in to the Evil One, and I am impoverished. Using my gifts promotes harmony and freedom and empowers me to become the person God created me to be. When I stifle God's energy through me, I become angry, jealous, and petulant.

As I attempt to live creatively, I am reminded again and again that my gifts, like the prayer of the heart, are not given to me for my own fulfillment or actualization. Rather, God bestows

Himself and His gifts in order that I might give with open hands as He has so generously given to me. As I am faithful to meditation and to the study of Scripture, I cannot hold His life or His gifts to myself.

In meditation, the conditions are set up to foster creativity. The process of allowing the presence of Christ to release imagination and intuition, and then to inspire the logical steps for bringing what has been imagined to fruition, can free the servant to let God do what He chooses. Meditation courts and feeds creativity.

I believe that God could do His work without any one of us. However, He has chosen to do His work through human instruments, and as long as He allows me to live on this earth, I assume that His work through me is not finished. When I have completed the work He has for me to do, I want to be able to hear Him say, "Well done, good and faithful servant."

Using creativity is an affirmation of God's life within me, an expression of hope. Responding to the call of God, bringing all of my life before Him, is one of the ways I show my trust in the Creator of the stars and the sun, the mountains and the flowers. Allowing myself the role of co-creator gives me a place to belong.

Christ is the wellspring of all inspiration, and so it is to Him I am to turn. I can trust God to give me the resources and the time I need to do His work. When I am faithful, His faithfulness is released in full measure, and then I discover a new element—joy. The Joy of knowing Christ fills every part of life with something beyond my understanding.

* * *

What does Scripture tell us about joy?

The first recorded miracle of Jesus in the gospel of John took place at a Jewish wedding feast where he turned water into wine. He participated wholly in the celebration and gave to the joy of the others who were present.

In the parable of the Prodigal Son, Jesus told the story of a lavish party thrown to celebrate the return of a wayward son. The elder brother, who could not come to the party because of his own jealousy and brokenness, was the one who missed out on the joy that was freely available for him.

As Jesus was entering into the last days of his life on earth, he prayed for his disciples and for all disciples to come. His petitions were for union with the Father, joy, protection, and usefulness. The sequence of those petitions is significant (John 17:11-17).

Friendship with Christ is the first priority and is basic for the qualities that follow. Out of that intimate, love relationship, joy is a logical consequence. Jesus knew, as he prayed for his disciples, that if they did indeed come into fellowship with him and exhibit the kind of full-fledged joy that he gives, there would be opposition from the world, and so he prayed not that his disciples would be protected from the world or taken out of it into a kind of insulated, holy huddle, but that they would be protected from anything that would destroy that union and joy. Then, out of that dynamic partnership, usefulness would naturally flow.

Many of us, brought up in the work ethic of our churches, have tried to get the union by our works. We have tried to exhibit joy we didn't have or have hoped to earn joy by working hard. While joy comes through giving myself away, I become burned out *unless that joy and my service flow from my friendship with Christ.*

In that petition for joy, Jesus requested *His* joy, fully established, permanent and consistent for his disciples. That joy was to be the norm for the Christian and not the exception. It was to be the baseline of experience, the means and not the end, the cause instead of the effect.

In my own journey, I am discovering that the joy which results from a daily communion with the Father is a powerful energy source and that regular communion with God raises the baseline of my joy. The more I know Him, the more I experience that deep inner well of joy that is not dependent on external circumstances. This joy is present even in the midst of suffering and sorrow; it is a motivating power even in discouragement and dismay.

Staying centered in the joy of God's presence also helps me choose those activities and outlets which are within God's design for my abilities and energies. For me, staying centered is a prerequisite for creative use of time management. While I could choose to do any number of things in the world, I am most efficient and productive when I do those things which line up with my call. A few forays into areas outside my abilities have proven, miserably, the mistake of trying to do what I am not created to do. Like the Prodigal Son, I returned home from these experiences, eager to get back to my own expression of my call.

That condition of joy which is based in God's presence is let loose in careers and jobs which bring meaning and purpose to the world. These jobs are not necessarily "religious," but as they are performed, the love of God transforms both the worker and the work.

James Herbert and Dwain Dodson, both pediatricians, are obvious instruments of God as they tend newborn babies and care for sick children. Their compassion and gentleness and their delight in their work make it clear that each of these godly men is doing what he was created to do. They exhibit in their medical practice a deep reverence for life and for God.

Charlotte Caffey has used her secretarial skills to bring order into my world, and she sees her tasks as ministry and mission. She sees her role as one of service, of smoothing out rough places for others, of making it easy for others to do their work. And she does it, as she says, out of love.

Ruthi Seefeldt takes disorganized pieces of information and, seemingly without effort, organizes and produces exactly what is needed. Her clear, sharp mind sees right to the core of a problem. Then she goes to work on finding solutions. It all takes place with the joy of doing what she is supposed to be doing. Her work and worship and play are often simultaneous expressions of that joy.

Ken Medema, a contemporary Christian musician who is blind, expresses Christ's love through his music, and his enjoyment of the process electrifies the concert hall. Another friend uses her needlework shop and skills to express God's love. Those who are gifted to work with their hands express their prayer in the act of producing a product as well as in the product itself, and there is joy in the process. Others perform acts of mercy out of a centeredness in

God's grace. People prepare meals with a sense of working with the parts of God's creation to feed and nourish His children, and the blessing is for the giver and the one who receives. Those artisans, craftsmen, and workers who have yielded the parts of their lives to God seem to have an inner spring of joy and serenity which overflows onto all those recipients of their labor. They do what they could not do on their own power, and they make the world more beautiful with their acts of grace.

*   *   *

"Where do you get your ideas?" the woman's voice on the end of the telephone inquired, and then she asked if I would talk about the process to her third-grade class.

It seemed a simple enough question, and I was eager to describe the creative process to a group of third graders—in fifteen minutes or less, of course.

I could explain about the dozens of snatches of paper with hastily written ideas, scribbled onto napkins in a restaurant, store receipts in the car, or note pads in the middle of the night. I could describe the ever-seeking mind, my practice of "going to school" wherever I am, and the need to develop keen powers of observation. I could talk to them about harvesting each day's experiences for stories.

They would understand something about a sense of play and adventure. Third graders know what it is to throw themselves into something with abandon.

Third graders understand surprise and mystery, so I could tell them how ideas sometimes emerge from some unconscious anteroom, just as my pen opens the door to my craft.

But would they understand how closely the act of creativity is related to the act of prayer, and that both are acts of adoring the Creator and of letting His action and life flow through the believer? That moment of unhindered joy is the process, which I have come to call *Creative Silence*. It has been both the object of my search and the shaper of my days and nights for several years. *How would I communicate this process to third-graders?* I wondered.

Turning inward to encounter God has not always been immediately "productive" (in an era which places high value on productivity), and sometimes my endeavors might be called failures (in a culture which worships achievement). Many times I have felt that I was spinning my wheels or that nothing "happened," but *never* have these been wasted times, for it has often been in the later moments of work that God has most clearly broken through my doubtings and my wanderings to reveal Himself as the ultimate reality—the only security in a madly turning world. It has been in the silence that I have been confronted with the only source of unconditional love, so I have learned that to search in any other relationship for that kind of love is not only fruitless, but sin.

The joy is that the daily discipline of drawing apart for the silent prayer, the practicing of the fundamentals, creates the silence I can carry around with me into the duties and responsibilities, the human encounters, the wonderings and wanderings about the earth. Then, because I have practiced beforehand and am sensitized to the activity of a loving and gracious God who longs to have fellowship with me, the music breaks loose at the most unexpected times, and I meet God in the most unexpected places, in the most remarkable ways, expressing what I have learned in those moments of holy fellowship.

As I allow God to express Himself through me, the simple, mundane and routine chores of life are transformed into a new dimension. Truly, it is possible to "chop wood and carry water" with a sense of divine purpose. It is possible to perform menial tasks with an awareness of God's presence working through the work. Acts of service become blessings; responsibilities carried out in God's love become prayers.

Carrying that silence, that inner sanctuary, with me and pausing now and then throughout the day to affirm that Presence, makes life adventure, mystery, and celebration. I see things more clearly. I feel life more deeply. And I live and love more fully.

Somehow, I think the third graders understood, for life has not yet taught them to forget. They knew what I was talking about when I talked to them about getting so caught up in their play that they forgot what time it was. They understood what I meant when I talked about paying attention to nature, for they still get sidetracked by things that catch their attention on the way home from school.

* * *

My car slipped on the steep, snowy hill leading down into the Frio Canyon. At each curve, I aimed my wheels away from the drop-off and toward the rocky banks. Shivering in cold fear, I watched dusk suddenly drop itself all around me. Josie, my dog and my sole companion, panted beside me.

I prayed for strength and safety. I prayed that Ken Cave, the camp director, would be in his cabin. I prayed that the road to the bottom of the hill would be shorter than I remembered.

Finally, we slipped to a stop at the lighted house. I rang the bell, expecting a warm welcome. Instead, I was met by a surprised couple. Ken and Jo Cave obviously hadn't gotten word that I was coming to stay in one of the houses at the HEB Foundation Camp. I had come to see if I had the courage to let my creativity loose on paper. I was compelled to finish a major writing project, but I was also terrified that I couldn't do what I wanted to do.

"Did you come down that hill?" the startled director asked. Dimly, I wondered how else I might have made that journey. Only later did I realize that *no one* had been able to go up or down the steep, narrow dirt road since the snow had fallen.

"Lodestar is frozen up," Ken said. "The pipes are all frozen."

"What about the Quiet House?" I inquired, forgetting for a moment that my favorite retreat place was even higher up the canyon than Lodestar. Its pipes, of course, would be the first to freeze.

"We had to evacuate the couple that was to be there this week when all this bad weather started."

My heart was sinking; fatigue rolled through my body. Had I misread the clues? Was it my stubborn self-will that had brought me here? Or was God really leading?

"You could stay in the River House," Ken said after pondering the situation for a few moments. Relieved and weary, I quickly got directions and inched my car one hundred slick yards to this welcomed haven. Back and forth I trudged through the snow, unloading books and paper, food and clothes. The canyon wore an eerie white silence; out of the silence of my heart, I prayed that my creativity could flow.

Ken and Jo had no idea how significant my journey was, for I had pulled off nothing short of a miracle to break away from my family and work schedule for six days to complete this manuscript. I had been working on the project for two years now, and it was time to bring it all together. I wasn't sure I had what it took; writer's block had choked and frozen my efforts for the past months, and yet somehow, I believed God had been in the inspiration, and I wanted to believe He was in the setting-apart of this week.

The next morning broke sunny and warm in typical Texas fashion. I walked down to the familiar Frio River and climbed onto one of the big sitting rocks along the bank. The river where my children had waded in gleeful celebration of summer camp was icy now. The bluff down which happy campers had rappelled wore big icy whiskers.

I sat on the rock and remembered the happy times of solitude and creativity at Laity Lodge. Suddenly, across the river, one of the icicles gave in to the sun's warmth and crashed to the river, to be followed by another and still another. All through the day, I heard the splash of icicles and the river flowing on its way.

That's what happens in meditation. The warmth of God's love moves into the coldness of my heart to thaw my fears and melt my resistance to life. In union with Christ, I am loved into a new freedom; I am forgiven and cleansed and healed; and finally, God burns a call in my heart. As I give up using my energy to hold on to the controls of life and to maintain negative, harmful attitudes, energy is released to express my creativity. When I give up fighting life, the flow of God's love starts moving, and I want to express it in some positive, helpful way. Joy is then made visible and I sing, "Joy to the world. The Lord has come." In creativity, joy comes to me . . . and I pass it on.

EXERCISE

Be very still and quiet.

Picture yourself as a little child, before the lights in your heart were snuffed out by the cares and worries of life. Picture yourself free and happy, running unself-consciously through a green meadow.

Stop and remember what it was you wanted to be and do before you knew there were limitations and restrictions on what was possible.

Ask God to reveal His call to you. Sit quietly in the silence, listening for His voice. Let Him tell you how He wants to unleash His joy through you.

Be willing to wait patiently for the unfolding of His original design. If the call isn't clear, continue to seek His fellowship and eventually you will be able to hear it. He has told you before, but you may have closed Him out.

If you have already defined your call, ask God for the courage to have the freedom to do the work He's called you to. Thank Him for the opportunity to be His instrument.

Seek first the rule and reign of God; everything else, in its time, will fall into place.

C·h·a·p·t·e·r F·o·u·r

CHRIST WITHIN

*"It is not the remembrance of what Jesus has
once done to me,
but the living experience of what He is now to me,
that will give me the power to act like Him.
His love must be a present reality,
the inflowing of a life and power in which I can
love like Him."*
—Andrew Murray

*". . . I count all things to be loss
in view of the surpassing value
of knowing Christ Jesus my Lord."*
—Philippians 3:8, NASB

*"Now this is eternal life: that they may know you,
the only true God, and Jesus Christ whom
Thou hast sent."*
—John 17:3, NIV

"What does that phrase *in Christ* mean?" The question from
the serious young woman interrupted the flow of conversation.

I had been buzzing along, thoroughly enjoying leading a spiritual growth group at our local Pastoral Care and Counseling Center, when this participant's question made me realize I had been

tossing out well-worn phrases I had always taken for granted and sent me seeking new answers.

To be "in Christ," I discovered, is to be a *practicing* Christian. It is to live with the awareness of Christ's presence both within and without and to be committed to following His pattern of life. It requires surrendering to His power day by day, knowing His mind and heart on a deep, personal, and vital level. That surrender occurs as I make daily, conscious contact with Him through meditation, responding to the love He is always extending.

By spending time with the Lord in meditation, I come to know His mind and heart much the same as I have come to know my husband's over the years. Most of the time, I know what my husband wants. I know what he values and what he dislikes, and I can sense when he is displeased, even if he tries to cover up his feelings. I know what will make him comfortable and happy, and many times, I can predict his decisions . . . but not always.

When Martus Miley and I first married, I knew lots of facts about him. I could tell you some of his history and his educational background. I knew about a few of his likes and dislikes, but the knowledge I possessed on our wedding day in 1967 was meager compared to the knowledge of each other we share today.

My intimacy with Martus has grown through years of spending time together, of struggling through the clashes of will, of daring to be open and vulnerable with him. I've learned about this fellow human being as I've watched him work; I've seen his character as he solves problems and as he plays. Many things have taught me who he is—watching him in his roles as father and son, seeing the way he handles money and time and gifts and interruptions. He is my good friend . . . because I have walked alongside him now for more than twenty years. And so it is with the Lord. We learn about Him by spending time with Him.

Before Christ's death, he told his disciples important things, and one of those was that they were now to be his friends. "You are my friends, if you do what I command. I no longer call you servants, because a servant does not know his master's business. Instead, I have called you friends, for everything that I learned from my Father I have made known to you" (John 15:14–15, NIV). Meditation, for those of us on this side of the resurrection, is the process of being friends with the Risen Christ. As I spend time nurturing that friendship, the Holy Spirit forges a relationship with me and helps me to live "in Christ."

In fact, the sole objective of Christian meditation is not silence or emptiness but union and friendship with Christ. The point of meditation is to be filled with more and more of the presence of Christ. Just as our intimacy with others grows with time and nurturing, so does our friendship with Christ.

Jeanne Guyon recognizes this when she writes, "Jesus Christ is the Eternal Word. He, and He alone, is the source of new life to you. For you to have new life, He must be communicated to you. He can speak. He can communicate. He can impart new life. And when He desires to speak to you, He demands the most intense attention to His voice."[5]

But for God to give us new life, He must be the center of our meditation. Everything I learned about the history of meditation and from my own practice convinced me of the necessity of making Christ my focal point. It is a conviction grounded in my childhood training. One of my earliest memories is of my minister father proclaiming the centrality of Christ. I didn't know what he meant for many years, but the truth came home to me as I ventured into my adult years and encountered numerous forces vying for that central place in my priorities.

Even when I was not aware of it, I could be influenced by the voice of tradition and others' expectations. I was so trained and conditioned in my role as minister's wife that I might act in accordance with that role instead of as a redeemed child of God. The voice of my own needs for security, recognition, or affirmation might speak more loudly than the impression of God's guidance.

And, so, I concluded that any other method of meditation except that which centers in Christ will ultimately fall short. Any other technique will lack life-changing power. Any gimmick, trick, or promise will lead you to look only to yourself for strength and transformation, and because you are finite, you will finally run aground. No mere chanting of "ohm" will provide satisfaction for the Christian meditator!

Friendship with Christ is a lofty goal, but what does it mean? How do I live out the "oneness" of the vine and the branches as I run my carpools, pay my bills, and meet the ever-present deadlines and demands of life?

Rodney Gibson, a retired Presbyterian minister and beloved counselor, attempted to answer that question for a friend of mine as she began her journey out of despair. "Study the Gospels," he said. "Soak yourself in the life of Christ, for that alone is your source of power."

Years later, I stood with Rodney and Amalia Gibson in their lake house. By this time, the effects of time and disease had crippled his body and depleted his physical strength. Every act—speaking, eating, moving—was difficult for him. However, as the three of us stood together to pray, he grasped my hand with an incredible strength. And when he began to pray with such fervor and clarity, I had to peek to see if this was the same man who had, moments before, been passive in a wheelchair, barely able to move without Amalia's aid.

"How good it is to know you, Lord," his voice rang out. And I saw the light of Christ in the faces of these two faithful followers who had spent their lifetime "soaking up the Gospels." These loving, gentle folks had been grasped by the love of Christ and had then extended that love to hungry, yearning hearts such as mine.

Seeing their example gave me encouragement. If studying the life of Christ was the route to this kind of joy, I was ready. I began to read both the Gospels and books about Christ. My hunger to know Him was enormous, and He honored my search by revealing Himself to me.

My search to know Christ more intimately led me to look more intently at the facts of His life. Then as I spent time pondering those facts, deeper meanings seemed to unfold. Scripture led the way, yielding truth and guidance as I studied the incredible story of Jesus of Nazareth.

I surprised myself one Sunday when I announced to the church's Singles Class, which I was teaching at the time, that we would study the life of Christ in Sunday School! Each week as I would sit down to prepare for the next week's lesson, my stomach would sink. Who did I think I was that I could teach such a subject? What did I know? Didn't I need seminary training for *this* job?

But I had made a commitment. I had publicly announced that this would be our study, and so I would open my books, praying that God would forgive my audacity, but honor my search. Later, I would get up from my work knowing that *this* study, this delving into the life of the one I called Savior and Lord, would change my life. I knew I could never be the same after this encounter with Christ.

In fact, it is that same love for Christ and desire to place Him at the center of life that has also moved others to service. It is the motivation behind the work of the Church of the Saviour in the ghettos of Washington, D.C., and behind the creation of a quiet place for pilgrims at Laity Lodge in the Hill Country of Texas. I see Christ's love in the actions of faithful, searching Christians in Southland Baptist Church who are attempting to know what it means to be the body of Christ on earth. I see that love in the face of our pediatrician, Dwain Dodson, as his gentle hands minister to an infant's medical needs and in the extravagant, wall-size stitchery art of my friend, Sandra Hulse. Her wonderful art is a celebration of God's love and an expression of her faith and joy in existence, and it reminds me of God's generous and impractical love.

That's the kind of love I want! Now that I have experienced it, nothing else will satisfy me. Just the knowing that this kind of love is possible keeps me moving toward the light, choosing to open myself up over and over to the Christ-life. I have discovered that His life within me becomes like new wine, creating a joyous, effervescent source of power which breaks down the barriers of my old life.

When I choose Christ as the focus, the stillpoint, and the organizing principle of my life, I am on safe ground. A lighted candle may indeed serve to help me train my power of concentration or to point me beyond its flickering light to the true Light of the World, but it is only a vapor. Nothing else can transform me but the power of Christ in me.

The resounding message of the biblical record, culminating in Revelation, is that Christ is the only one worthy of my worship. He is the Alpha and Omega . . . and it is He who invites us to know Him, to follow Him, and to become like Him.

In Jesus, God is brought close to us; for by seeing how He lived life, how He approached conflict and suffering, how He treated sinners, we can know how he treats us. We see His miracles and believe they can happen to us; we know He healed, and we want the same for our sick and broken world.

In Jesus, God turned the world's view upside down and positioned His kingdom within His followers. Through meditation, I affirm that kingdom, explore its possibilities, and live out its power.

The simplest ways are often the most difficult; my friends who are in Alcoholics Anonymous say, "The hard way is the easy way." I tend to want something elaborate or spectacular to save me, and I *surely* want something quick and easy. Or I say, "Yeah, well, that worked for you, but I'm a different case." I may sit by the well, knowing its waters could heal, yet all the time hoping for some new cure. *Then* I could *really* believe!

The way to know Christ, to have fellowship and union with Him, is very simple—spend time with Him as you would a close friend. If that's hard to imagine, *pretend* He's there with you. Read the stories and parables in the Gospels and pretend *you were there.* Meditate, mull over, chew on His teaching until you can "work" them in the parts of your life. Ask Christ to reveal Himself to you; picture His life actually residing in you. Give your imagination to Him in prayer, abandoning it to Him, and ask Him to use it to teach you what it means to "abide in Christ."

I learned another method of getting to know Christ one cold December day as I sat fireside with a renowned teacher of spiritual direction and several other seekers at an advent retreat. In a gentle sort of way, Bob Dougherty led us to Luke's account of the annunciation of Christ's coming, teaching us to "pray the Scriptures." As we read and re-read each passage, we began identifying with the doubt of Zacharias and the acceptance of Mary. We began to taste and see, smell and hear the Scriptures, feeling the heartbeat of God's Word, as we recognized in a more intense way the power and meaning of Christ's birth. That ancient method of praying the scriptures is a useful tool in knowing Christ.

"Focus!" commands the karate master in the popular Karate Kid movies. "You must gaze at what you want to imitate."

In the book *Like Christ*, Andrew Murray also describes this technique. He tells of a classroom of children who were asked to look at a picture carefully. Then they were to close their eyes and visualize the picture in their imagination, or their "mind's eye."

Murray calls us to use the same technique with the Gospels. He encourages us to become so familiar with Christ's life that we can "see" Him. Try using your imagination to be there in the stories with Christ. Hear the words that He directed to long-ago persons as directed to you. Allow his questions to others, such as "Who do you say I am?" or "What do you want me to do for you?" to probe deep into your heart.

Another method for knowing Christ is to select one of the names of Christ and spend time pondering who this human with divine being is to you. Do you need "the great physician?" How can he be "the good shepherd" to you? How is he "Friend," "Teacher," "Master," "Redeemer," "Savior," or "Lord?" Mull these phrases and functions over in your meditation time and allow His Spirit to teach you what He wants you to know.

Jesus *said* that it was possible to know Him. Claim the power by persistent practice and through faithful study of His work. Give yourself permission to relax into the assurance that He *will* honor His word.

It is not enough, however, just to gaze at the object of our faith, to enjoy the holy communion with the Faithful Friend, or to snuggle down into the security of abiding in Him. The other part of union with Christ is obedience.

Obedience and abiding go hand in hand; they are two essential parts of the life of meditation. It is in obeying that the union with Christ is verified and validated; it is in walking with Christ that I gain the guidance, strength, courage, and wisdom to live.

I find the call to obey Christ to be equally as challenging as that to abide in Him. Both propel me into thought patterns and actions counter to my natural instincts and to my culture, for the whole life of Christ and the Christlike life *are* at odds with the self-centered culture we have evolved.

I continually bump into parts of my life which are out of harmony with Christ's loving intent. Each day, I see new areas which do not conform to His standards, but the Good News is that He is walking with me and is at work to make His life more and more my life. It is progress that counts, and He is infinitely patient.

The important thing, again, is a willing, teachable spirit and a simple, childlike willingness to do what is right and pleasing to the Father. And that comes as a gift of grace, through time and the continuing practice of the presence of God.

As I practice the reign and rule of God in my life—often *pretending* that I'm able to do a given task, sometimes *hoping* that God is indeed in charge, always *wanting* the higher road of His call even when I drift back to my self-willed, miserably comfortable ways—I learn what it means for Christ to be both Savior and Lord. *Through meditation, it is possible to set out on the journey of knowing Christ; to come to understand, though gradually, His character; to know what He will do and what His resources are.*

While it is important to know the facts about Christ's life and to understand the depths of the mystery that He is the best picture of God, it is even more important to internalize His character, so that His life can perfect mine. This relationship is an ever-changing, ever-growing one, just as are my human friendships.

Jesus Christ is the only one who can lead me to freedom. He can do work through me that I could never do on my own power. He can carve out a new, courageous heart for me, filling it with His love, and He can perfect His life in me. *He would never have called us to friendship, to perfection, to do His work if He hadn't also provided the means to make it happen.*

The claims and promises of Christ are as astounding as His life, and I must *choose* to bet my life that He really was who He said He was. Meditating on His life, pretending that He really does live in me even when I can't intellectually grasp that truth or *feel* His presence, will finally enable me to recognize His presence. Meditating on Christ opens the door to union, to that friendship which is beyond words. Affirming with my words and my heart that He lives in me opens my capacity for that reality. Finally, I come to a place of such surrender that I am aware, deeply and surely, that it is He who is my prayer; indeed, His spirit prays in me.

＊　＊　＊

An artist, deeply focused on her medium and centered in the process of creativity, is oblivious to all but the process flowing unhindered through her. Later, astonished with the product, she exclaims, "Did that come from me?" and gives thanks to God for being allowed to be the instrument of the art.

A small child, moved in worship by the reality of God's enfolding love, describes the experience as "God's hugging me for the day." She never doubts either God's love or the experience; she knew He was right there with her, helping her begin the day.

A contemplative encounters the living Christ in his daily prayers, and, for that moment, the world stands in awesome, exquisite stillness. From that encounter the strength and grace to meet the challenges of a new day flow gently, but surely, into action.

Our pattern for the inner, private journey is an infallible one. Our Lord, the very Son of God, drew away on a regular basis to pray, and He affirmed, "I and the Father are one." Out of that drawing away, Jesus stayed in touch with who He was and what He was to be about. The prayers of Christ reaffirmed His dependence on His Father, and out of that vibrant, creative silence, the power of redemption was born.

Because Christ was firmly and irrevocably centered within the will of His Father, He was able to perform miracles and teach the multitudes, heal the sick and turn water into wine. Finally, His union with God enabled Him to confront Calvary and, ultimately, to overcome death.

Meditation. Practicing the presence of God. Inner stillness. The prayer of the heart. Inner light. Contemplation. Friendship with the Christ of Calvary. Reflective living.

All of these terms reflect an inner yielding to the Father, a movement toward union with the Holy Other. Part of this yielding is learning to listen. It is acceptance, abandonment, and surrender of the small everyday parts of life. It is the constant recognition and the daily living out of the reality that we are living in the ocean of God's love. Instead of trying to escape life and its predicaments, we are given the power to live redemptively and creatively within them. Whereas I have been prone to analytical problem-solving and preoccupation with my own inner needs until I am literally going around in circles, meditation enables me to transcend my situation and escape the self-centered mazes. Through meditation I am filled with God's Spirit. Christian meditation does not mean "emptying my mind" or achieving a state of nothingness. Instead, I am ushered into the Source of life itself. Christ lives within me.

EXERCISE

Come into the silence reverently, gently, not rushed, not forcing an experience.

As you breathe deeply, affirm, "Christ in me, the hope of glory," or "He lives in me." Another affirmation is "Christ loves me and gave Himself for me," or "Christ loves me, and I love Him, too. What joy."

These ancient affirmations will aid you in "centering," placing yourself in the center of God's care and placing Him in the center of yourself.

Once you have centered your thoughts on Christ begin the process of imaging.

Picture yourself again in a sunny meadow, walking calmly toward a cool, still lake. Feel a gentle breeze on your face. Imagine the song of a bird above you. Enjoy the goodness of God in a deep blue sky, a patch of wildflowers. Hear the honk of the geese, the quacking of the ducks. See yourself sitting down beside the lake on a huge, warm rock. Take off your shoes and feel the cool water lick your toes; squash the mud around your toes.

Suddenly, you see a figure crest the gentle hill to your left and begin to walk toward you. You are completely at peace, unafraid of this stranger.

He comes toward you; you ask him to sit down. When he turns to look at you, you realize He is the Savior, the Risen Christ, the Son of God.

Take a few moments to feel how it is to be sitting with Messiah! Picture, in your imagination, His tender eyes. Don't turn away from their probing. See the love and compassion in His eyes. Feel the warmth of His delight in you. If you want to, picture your hand reaching out to His.

In the silence, listen to your inner talking. Be aware of whatever thought comes to your consciousness.

Ask Him whatever you want. Ask Him anything.

Tell Him what is hurting you; tell Him your fears, your cares, your joys, your happiness.

Sit in the silence a few more minutes and then gently pray, "Speak, Lord, for thy servant heareth."

Then wait for the silence to bring His word.

What is it Christ is saying to you?

LETTING GO . . .

"Be still, and know that I am God."
—Psalm 46:10, KJV

*"Casting all your cares upon him,
for he careth for you."*
—1 Peter 5:7, KJV

*"There is a divine plan of good at work in my life.
I will let go and let it unfold."*
—Ruth P. Freedman

*"I don't know who —or what —put the question,
I don't know when it was put. I don't even
remember answering.
But at some moment I did answer yes to
Someone —or Something —
and from that hour I was certain that
existence is meaningful
and that, therefore, my life, in self-surrender, had a goal."*
—Dag Hammerskjøld

The hospital room was filled with tension. Since early morning, my father had been waiting to take the test which would
reveal his condition. With as much support as we could muster,

my mother and sister and I were overseeing the long wait. Hospital delays had prolonged our vigil for four hours, and our earlier composure grew ragged as we waited for the test and its verdict. Was my father's condition provoked by a brain tumor, a blood clot, or an aneurysm?

Blinded by double vision and unable to stand, my strong and vital father waited patiently in the chair beside his bed to be taken for an arteriogram. We had been told the test might provoke another stroke, or even his death, and so our waiting was filled with anxiety.

Finally, the pleasant, calm nurse we had already come to love, came with the release papers for Daddy to sign. As she dutifully read the risks and possibilities to him, his pent-up anxiety gave way to a rush of tears. He looked up at her as she read, his face as trusting as a child's.

"Do you understand, Dr. Ball?" she inquired, handing him a pen and guiding his hand to the paper.

With a childlike gesture, he brushed away his tears. "Yes," he said through sobs, "and what I don't understand is all right."

Now my own tears came unchecked, and I silently called on my heavenly Father as the nurse helped Daddy onto the gurney which would take him to the testing place.

"Now, Dr. Ball," the nurse chided, "your faith has been so strong."

"And it will hold. It will hold," he said, allowing her to ease him down for the long ride down the hospital corridor.

"That's the way he's lived his whole life," I said to my sister, and we clung to his faith as ours wavered.

My father's childlike surrender didn't begin in that hospital room, nor did what would prove to be a stroke on his fifty-ninth wedding anniversary change his faith—it only altered his lifestyle. His trust and faith had been carved out in the preceding years as he had remained faithful to his call. God worked an act of grace in this man during his youth, and he had never strayed from that commitment.

Perhaps that example in the faith of my father made it possible for me to accept the idea of abandonment to God. Maybe the life of surrender that I had seen in both my father and mother gave me the picture of what yielding to God was all about.

However, I was to learn that I must walk through the process of surrender on my own. No one could do it for me, and when I decided, in my adult life, to surrender to God, I had only the vaguest understanding of what that decision would entail. I had been taught, however, that giving oneself to God was the thing to do, and so on I trudged.

"I can tell you how you begin to let go of what ails you," my friend declared. "What you do is summed up in the first three steps of AA."

She had my interest, for while alcohol and drugs were not my addictions, I was vaguely aware that the Twelve Steps of AA could be used to help heal all sorts of broken places in one's life.

My friend went on to show me that the key to surrender is admitting that "I can't," but that "God can," and "I'm going to let Him." I found that same formula in Psalm 51: I have sinned. God can forgive. I'm going to let Him heal me.

*　　*　　*

Over one hundred college students were sprawled before me at Singing Hills Camp. Outside, crickets chirped and the Frio River flowed lazily down through the canyon. These college seekers could barely contain their youthful excitement at being away on retreat. Their antics had livened up the evening meal, but now it was time for The Program . . . and I was on.

I looked out at the upturned faces and began to speak of surrender to God. What would happen if these youth could be convinced that surrender to God would bring them what they were looking for? Could we—their leader and I—channel their energies toward God before they surrendered their minds, bodies, and wills to lesser gods?

Soon one young man objected. "If I can't trust my friends, whom I can see, how do you expect me to trust God, whom I cannot see?"

It was a fair question, I had to admit, and I groped for the right words to spark the flickering faith in the disillusioned college student.

"You tell me to abandon myself to God. You gotta know that my father abandoned my mother before I was even born!" He literally spat the words *abandon* and *father* toward me, his face contorted with an anguish which was all too familiar.

I recognized that the challenge was mine, but I wasn't quite prepared for the jolting honesty of his statement. If I thought the surrender of my will was difficult, I had only begun to encounter the difficulties of convincing others to surrender theirs! But I couldn't avoid these questions because they are the first barrier to true surrender. Surrender does indeed become a problem when we make God in the image of frail human beings; regretfully, too many know the heartache of a cruel, absent, or indifferent earthly parent. No wonder "giving oneself" to the Unseen is difficult. We see God with limited vision, colored by the distortions and disappointments of the past.

Surrender is especially difficult in this era of self-sufficiency. None of us is anxious to let go of our independence. To do so is risky; it evokes disturbing questions and unsettled feelings. Too often we are reminded of humans who have let us down, times we have failed, or petitions we made which were not granted. At a deep level, we hold on to our fears and doubts.

> God will take care of me except when I . . . (you fill in the blank).

> What if He looks away just as I am about to fall off a cliff?

> What if He counts the hairs on everyone else's head but mine?

> What if He doesn't save my marriage or heal my child?

> What if I lose my job or go bankrupt? What about surrender then?

> Besides, doesn't He get tired of my straying away and then coming back and straying again? What if He says I've blown it once too often or that *this* is the one sin He won't forgive?

But Scripture assures us that God is not going to betray us as human parents and friends so often do.

How easily we forget the story of the Prodigal Son and how his father raced joyfully to meet him, lavishing love and mercy and joy on the son and then throwing the party to celebrate the return.

And how quickly we forget Christ's tender offer of living water to the Samaritan woman. (That was "back then," you say. What does that have to do with me now?)

God is big enough and loving enough to accept even you and me. His goodness and greatness are infinitely more powerful than our badness or our littleness.

I've discovered that the key to living, practicing, and expressing the presence of God is in that surrender of all that I know of myself to all that I know of God. Surrendering myself to God is a process of losing myself to find myself, an emptying of all that is old and harmful so that I may be filled with power and peace, joy and love. Surrendering is letting go of all that is not worthy of me and taking on a new life. Surrender is part of the work of meditation; it is the challenge of practicing the presence of God. It is trusting God completely.

Whenever I think back to my first awareness of the concept of surrender, I remember a bleak winter evening, deep in the Frio Canyon ten years ago, when another group of college students gathered at the HEB Camp to participate in a trust exercise. Of course, everyone was uncomfortable, trying to hide behind giggles and jokes.

The retreat leader asked the college students to form a circle. One slightly willing subject, a young man whose childhood and youth were scarred by abuse and neglect, stood in the center of the circle. He was told to fold his arms, keeping his body rigid, and then to fall backward into the arms of his peers.

Later, this same young man was lifted and carried on a "tour" of the camp area by six of these same people. After the experience, he said, "I was scared to death, but when we went through the door and down some steps, several hands came around my head to protect it. I think that's the first time in my life I've known what it was to trust."

If it's difficult to fall back into the arms of waiting humans, or to allow oneself to be carried through strange territory by un-named friends, of course it is difficult to fall back in the arms of God—*unless you practice that surrender, that trust, as a discipline of love in meditation.*

I have discovered that true union with God is possible only through surrender and that the act of giving up rights to oneself is an act of faith. God rewards that drawing near, that giving of all that you are, by building even more faith.

Surrender to God, practiced in the daily twists and turns of life, is affirming that God is the Creator and I am the creature. It is looking for His hand everywhere, believing that He is in control. Surrender is betting my life on the fact that Jesus Christ is who He says He is and that He will do what He says. I have found that the surrender of my life to the Lord of all of life is the only way to discover peace of heart and to release my creativity as a gift of healing.

Surrender is responding to His touch, hearing His call, saying yes to His beckoning. Surrender is becoming aware that He is moving in worship, in nature, in His people.

Surrender of my will is the most difficult of all the disciplines of the contemplative life. It is harder than spending ten minutes twice a day in silence. It is harder than keeping focused on His presence. It is harder than "serving" Him. And yet, it is the first step toward wholeness.

Surrender is not resignation. It is not shirking responsibility or turning my back on problems. It is turning toward God and releasing my tight grasp on life. It is giving Him permission to be who He is: God of the Universe and of me. It is cooperating with Him rather than fighting Him.

Meditation conditions the mind and heart to be willing and aware; it cultivates the soil in which surrender to the Author of Life can grow.

*   *   *

"Are you totally committed?" The source of the question was a sweet, young woman, and I could tell from the way she chirped the question that she was not so much testing me with this catch phrase as she was looking for someone to affirm her! It was obvious that she felt that she had surrendered her life totally to God.

That incident took place over ten years ago, but I've thought about that question many times in the intervening years. Even then, I had a shadowy understanding that surrender and commitment were much more a process of growth than a state to achieve.

I *was* committed, sort of, to God then, just as I was aware, to a degree, of myself and God. I had given my life to Him as a nine-year-old child, with whatever understanding I had at the time. As the years have worn on, however, I have discovered that He continues to move deeper and deeper into my life, uncovering new areas over which I try to exert control. New challenges and heartaches, as well as new expressions of giftedness have emerged; I have needed to bring each of these before the Father and relinquish them to Him.

Repeatedly, I surrender my will—my stubborn, stiff-backed will that thinks it knows best and insists on having its own way. I give God my mind and emotions, my body, my gifts, and my efforts. I give Him my time, my problems, and my joys, because I have learned that His lordship is the only one that works.

I have tried giving myself to other gods—the gods of education and knowledge, success and money, accomplishment and work. I have given good works First Place in my affection. I have tried to get other people to be god for me; I have even let the church assume top priority in my time and energy. I have placed my neck in other worldly nooses and yokes, but only the yoke of Christ grants me freedom.

Surrendering my will to His yoke is a constant process. As I continue to allow the presence of God to permeate the various parts of my life, I am understanding more clearly that anything or anyone, other than God, to whom I turn for meaning, purpose, or strength will ultimately disappoint me or destroy me. God affirmed the first commandment for my benefit; He knew I would never be whole as long as I worshiped anything or anyone besides

Himself. I have tried to fill my life with other people, pleasure, work, and acquisition, but these things only partially satisfy.

I am learning that that which is empty cannot fill me, and so I am able more and more to turn aside from dried up, empty wells of fame and fortune, success, power, and achievement to partake of the Living Water. I am learning that the God of Abraham, Joseph, and Isaac is indeed the Source of everything I need and that His intent is *always* for good.

That well-worn adage "practice makes perfect" is especially true of the surrender of life. As you practice surrender everyday, it will lead to trust and obedience; and obedience will lead to perfect peace.

The way of surrender is paved as I become acquainted with God. I can't very well keep on trusting my life to Someone I don't know, so I must build an adequate concept of God by studying His Word. As I learn about the ways He has dealt with others, I learn what to *expect* from Him. In meditation, I am not just emptying my mind. It is not to nothingness that I am called to yield, but to God.

Early in my adult years, while attending a Yokefellow Spiritual Growth Group, I heard the leader say, "God is continually broadcasting His love to you." That message cast in modern language got through to me. I could imagine the unseen, invisible sound and light rays of modern communication beaming their way through to me just as the sun's rays shine on me.

I pictured God shining His light and His presence on me. Soon, these mental efforts shifted to another level, and I began to *feel* the presence of God. I can't explain the process nor can I chart it, but there arose out of this affirmation the knowledge that God was all around me.

That sense of nearness made it easier for me to give myself to God, and the surrender made it possible for me to maintain an attitude of expectancy: *God will speak to me!* What I must do is give him my attention (surrender) so that I can recognize His presence! His presence will then create a sensitivity to His desires and activity.

I am learning to offer events and relationships to Him. Reading His word gives me an objective authority by which to measure my decisions. I test out my journey with other believers who are also seeking God's direction. Surrender enables me to be willing to let God's agenda be mine.

* * *

I had made it to the hammock first! Early birdsong was ushering up the morning as the rugged canyon wall faded into my vision. Delight filled my heart as I claimed the coveted watching place and prepared to do my morning devotion before the day's activities.

To be at Laity Lodge with Madeleine L'Engle as the guest speaker was a dream come true for me. It was Creativity Week, and I could hardly wait to see what lay in store for me.

I drew my feet under me, spread my journal and Bible out before me, and hoped I could balance in the hammock. The sounds of tennis balls rose from the courts below, and joggers passed behind me. A canyon wren played its scale and a tiny lamb followed its mother through the underbrush. What a gift to be here, I thought.

Breathing deeply, I began affirming my abandonment to God with my usual early morning prayer.

"Father, I abandon myself into your hands . . ."

Suddenly, as if on a bolt of lightning, new words popped into my head.

"Let go!" was the insistent urging.

"Do what?" I thought.

"Let go . . . let go . . . let go," the words kept coming.

I thought I had let go, but I was about to enter into a new stage of relinquishment. The surrender I had verbalized, theorized, and experienced in its merest beginning was about to become reality. Through the coming months, I would experience surrender at even deeper levels.

I would surrender my need to force results of events to fit my expectations. I would give up my need for others to behave according to my specifications. While I began to abandon my self-will run riot into God's hands, I also knew that this surrender would be a daily need for the rest of my life.

God was ushering me into a new training and testing through the leading of His still, small voice. I was to encounter Him more fully, but only as I walked into the shadows of unknowing and uncertainty. He was leading me into more fullness, but the price was to be extracted as I wrestled with my stubborn will.

Since that early morning encounter in the hammock at Laity Lodge, it seems that God has removed layer after layer of willfulness. My fear of others' control, my need to control, and my impulsive nature have been exposed in painful ways, but as each layer of sin has come into my awareness, I have experienced the healing grace of God. Somehow, God is nurturing His peace as I am letting go . . .

EXERCISE

As you settle down in your quiet space, exhale deeply, visualizing the tension flowing out of your fingertips and the ends of your toes.

With each inhalation, repeat, "I let go of _____," filling in the blank with whatever is troubling you.

As you sit in the silence, ask God to bring to your mind whatever you are clinging to which is keeping you from fully trusting Him.

Is there sin from your past which needs forgiving?

Is there a hurt which needs healing?

Are there broken relationships you need to release to God?

Are there dreams you need to offer to God?

Will you trust the outcome of your efforts to Him?

Will you let go of your fear? your need to control? your anger?

What is it God is willing to carry for you?

Will you give Him your will? your love?

C·h·a·p·t·e·r S·i·x

MY STUBBORN WILLFULNESS

"For the good that I wish, I do not do;
but I practice the very evil that I do not wish."
—Romans 7:19, NASB

"Surrender does not come easily."
—Gerald May

God must have been listening when I surrendered my life to Him, and apparently He took me quite seriously! I'm not sure I meant for my surrender to produce such radical changes.

I hadn't intended on changing my communication style or challenging my well-worn and familiar beliefs about God and how he works in the world. I didn't know that I would be led to deal with food obsessions or with the fact that I let other people control my decisions and my moods. I had no idea that surrender would force me to face my self-defeating patterns and to take steps to change. I wanted to be changed; I didn't necessarily want to change! This was more than I bargained for!

* * *

"Don't try to solve problems in your meditation time," Keith Hosey, my first spiritual director, advised. "Just sit in the silence and enjoy God!"

"Learn to play with God," he said, and with those instructions, he sent the Laity Lodge retreat participants out to spend a day of silence doing just that—an exercise we would repeat several times during the course of the retreat. I wondered if he had any idea how hard that was for this work-oriented Baptist, born and bred to the Baptist anthem "Toiling On." But I set out immediately to try to "waste time with God" by letting nature, selected scriptures, readings from the retreat sessions, and my own internal cues guide me to God's gift for that time.

From the very first, I ran into my resistance to change. I even ran into my resistance to feeling good or being happy; indeed, I battled with my resistance to God's love. I wanted to "work out" my problems, not relax. Meditation had forced me into a struggle, and the battle was difficult.

Getting still and quiet once again made a space in which I was forced to hear guidance I had tried to block with the mufflers of busyness. In the silence, I had to face myself, and with the knowledge I had gained in this part of my spiritual journey, I had to face my resistance to feeling good and being happy.

In the exercises of this particular retreat, I began to see how I had fought yielding to God. I saw, too, that my resistance to being creative and expressing my call was rooted in fear. With the help of Keith Hosey's lectures, I saw in new ways how I needed to relax and let go of my fears, my external motivators, and my need to control. The more I fought yielding to God, the more trouble I had being creative or productive in my work and in my relationships. So quickly I would forget that in the life of creativity and prayer, I needed to relax and let go. To "try harder" doesn't cut it.

I discovered that confronting the Holy One broke open an awareness of the broken places of my life. If I were to focus my life around the light of Christ and His truth, that Light would inevitably expose the darkness and deception. The decision to yield my life to Him forced me to face up to all the parts of my life which still needed to be brought under His Lordship.

In the weeks that followed the retreat at Laity Lodge, meditation on Christ's life turned loose a series of events. A new, demanding writing assignment from an unexpected source came in the mail.

An opportunity to test my new-found freedom and the communication that goes with freedom came within my family. New people came into my spiritual growth groups, challenging my mind and skills. Could I let go of fear and respond with faith and courage? Ways of mediating grace within our church family evolved, enabling me to act in strength I didn't know I had. The deaths of several close friends issued an invitation to enter into suffering at a new level instead of running away from the pain of others' loss. I learned that in order for His will to rule, my will had to be brought under His control . . . and there was my problem!

Confrontation with God exposed my brokenness in the very middle of family, work, and church life. I have wrestled and fought with myself and with God as He has pointed out the shackles which slow me down. To free me to live willingly yielded to Him, God has had to bring my willfulness, my fierce need and determination to control my life and Him, to my reluctant attention. Knowing that I have been called to "let go and let God" led me head-on into all the parts of my life to which I was clinging and to the idols to which I have clung for security—the idols of others' opinions, work and busyness, financial security, and other things to which I clung for comfort.

One of the clear indicators that my will is in control is a mounting frustration when things in life get complicated. I want to seize control and make things happen, and I first began to notice this about three years after I started trying to live the surrendered life. I was struggling with my call and my gifts and with the issues of financial stability. I felt afraid and began doubting my call and my decisions. Should I give up my present pathway of leading spiritual growth groups and writing, a pathway that had been blessed for sixteen years, and return to the public school classroom, which I had left twenty years before? How was I to interpret the events of my life? Should I take the easy way out or should I remain faithful to the present pathway?

"Please answer me, God!" I demanded. My footsteps beat a sharp staccato along my walking path. "I've got to have some answers!"

Faced with a crucial decision that would affect my family and me, I had turned to barking orders to God. It was not enough on this day that I had developed the awareness of His presence; it was time for action!

As I continued on my silent march, I carried on a heated debate with myself. If God had tried to break into the conversation, He would have had to send a lightning bolt.

"I thought I was doing the right thing, but now look at the mess I'm in," I worried. "I thought I was following Your guidance; after all, I did surrender my life to You! So what are You going to do now? I've tried to be obedient . . . I've tried to do Your will and Your work . . ."

God did nothing that day, much to my chagrin, and His silence deafened my ears. The next day, I found my way to my spiritual guide. Limping and whimpering, I told her all I could about my predicament.

Patiently, tenderly, she met with me each week, guiding me through the Song of Solomon, which I had never really read before, to come to an understanding of what it means to live with a heart receptive to the power and love of God. She helped me discover the ways I was trying to play God in my own life, how I was working so hard to earn His favors that I was beating myself down. She helped me see that in my zeal, I was returning to a life of law and legalism. ("Are you so foolish? After beginning with the Spirit, are you now trying to attain your goal by human effort?" Galatians 3:3, NIV). Carefully, she showed me how I was trying to do life all on my own strength and abilities, and so I began to learn at an even deeper level about the reality of depending on God, of claiming His provision moment by moment.

As I studied the Scriptures with my friend, I remembered a lesson I had learned only a few months before when I had been up against another event I couldn't control, change, or avoid. No matter how I had railed against God and ordered Him to "Do something!" or how often I had returned to my discipline of centering and submission, His silent majesty reigned.

Thinking I could manipulate Him to action, I had beaten against my loved ones with demands for them to do something (since it appeared that God was not going to!). Finally, one day, when I had sat down for my meditation time, I said, "Okay, God, You are the

God of this universe. All power is Yours, and if You wanted to, You could change this situation in the next instant. That's obviously not what You intend, and so I give up. You do with this situation and with all of us exactly what you want, and I'll cooperate!" (Wasn't that big of me to grant Him that permission?)

That statement of surrender "created a space" in my awareness for the conflict as I understood it to exist. I didn't know it then, but what I was doing was "letting it be." Then, and only then, could I begin to see how God really was at work.

As I yielded control of the situation to God and detached myself from it, my feelings of anger, resentment, and fear began to subside. As I observed the conflict dispassionately, it seemed to me that God moved to the helm, and I realized that He had changed my mind. He had changed my perception and interpretation, and I realized that I felt peace and hope for the first time in months. As I was given new eyes to see, nothing was changed, but everything was different.

I had finally come to the end of my strength in controlling those events. I'd tried all the ways I knew, all the time believing I was "entirely submitted" to God. But all the time I thought I was focusing on God, I was really intent on what I wanted Him to do. Now, at the end of my rope, I could do nothing other than let Him take over.

Out of that darkness of wrestling with God, I came to affirm that there is no valley so deep that God is not there. There is no night so dark but that the Light of the World shines brilliant and eternal. There is no hate so great that Love cannot overcome; there is no god which can finally triumph over the one true God.

In that encounter those several months before, I had fought the battle of trying to control others. I had tried to figure things out for all concerned; I thought that since I was consistently seeking God's presence, I knew what was best. Trusting more in my insights and intuition than in God's power, I tried to meddle my way into others' decisions. My reasoning only led to more willfulness.

In that battle, my frustration was that I knew I was right! My intuitions were proving to be correct, so why wasn't everyone falling into line? Over and over, conditions evolved just as I predicted, and the truth that I proclaimed was being revealed. Since no one was cooperating with me and my reasoning, I pouted. "I feel unheard," I would fret. "No one is listening to me!" I assumed my insights were straight from God; perhaps they were, but they were *not* God!

The danger and peril of spiritual growth is in becoming prideful. My insights did prove to be correct, and I took great joy, much later, in hearing, "You were right." However, the grave error for me was in assuming lordship over circumstances; what did it profit me, I began to see, if I did speak truth, but did not have love nor humility? What did it gain for me if I used my intuitive gifts or God's words to me as weapons against others?

The other pitfall I had not too gracefully fallen into was thinking that because God had led me to friendship with Him, I was somehow an especially selected dispenser of truth. I had begun trying to possess God; I was to learn that He is the Owner of all of us.

As if it weren't enough to do battle with my will, I have had to fight my need to control my own destiny. I had to learn that my gifts and abilities, my future and my opportunities are all His. I didn't think myself up nor did I make myself. I didn't invest myself with the gifts I have nor did I call myself into service. I am His, and He is Sovereign.

The spiritual pride that assumes that I can do with my life as I will because I am "trying to do the Lord's work," or because I am practicing some spiritual discipline, is a deathblow to God's working in and through me. It is an attitude which leads to all sorts of abuses of power and people.

My response to God had been, "Yes, but . . ." more often than simply, "Yes! Yes!" and always my intent was to stay in control. Assuming my willful control, I beat myself when things went "wrong" or when they became difficult; surely, I should have been able to manage myself better.

Now in the midst of still another testing period, and with the care of my guide, I began to meditate once again on God, using the Scriptures, instead of my desires, as my base. Gradually, as events beyond my control evolved, I had to confess that even my spiritual growth is out of my hands. God is the Designer and

Implementer of every facet of life, and it was He who had kept me returning to His presence through the long months of wrestling.

Through God's acts of grace in meditation, He has revealed harmful beliefs to which I have clung. Beliefs that have ruled my life, such as "I must please everyone" or "I've got to be perfect," have kept me from peace and serenity. "If he isn't pleased, I'm not okay" and "I've got to make everyone happy" are other beliefs which have also gotten in my way of knowing Christ. I have come to see through the painful circumstances of frustrated relationships and difficult choices that I beat myself mentally if I'm not perfect or if something goes awry. I've continued to live out old failures instead of allowing them to be forgiven and healed. Through His grace, however, God has led me to proclaim, "It is finished" when I attempt to pick up the sins and burdens of the past—and the past is what happened even a moment ago.

As I drew nearer to God through meditation, I discovered that my place in my marriage and family was changing. My friendships took on more meaning, and my gifts were being used in new ways. Over and over, I had to confess, "I can have no other gods before You" and "Thou art the Christ," as He showed me who was in charge of the universe.

Now as a result of these two major struggles and many lesser ones, I recognize that to surrender my will to God means I let go of problems, believing that those problems are allowed by God not to halt my progress, but to speed my way to Him. Of course, there are problems and pain in the Christian life! Of course, there is suffering and loss, absurdity and injustice because we live in a broken world. We must grapple with the forces of evil that are within and without, but as we give all of the brokenness to God, He alone can bring us to the perfection He had in mind when He made us.

During the seventeenth century, a spiritual advisor, Archbishop Fénelon, gave the following advice to a young woman who grappled with pain and suffering:

> The great Physician who sees in us what we cannot see, knows exactly where to place the knife. He cuts away that which we are most reluctant to give up. And how it hurts! But we must remember that

pain is only felt where there is life, and where there is life is just the place where death is needed. Our Father wastes no time by cutting into parts which are already dead . . . He wants you to live abundantly, but this can only be accomplished by allowing Him to cut into that fleshy part of you which is still stubbornly clinging to life.[6]

So, to grapple with my stubborn will, I abandon my imperfections to God. When I become aware of sin, I ask God to remove it and fill the void with His power. I give Him my pride, the rights of control I try to maintain over myself and my loved ones.

On my way to meet with friends, I abandon the forthcoming encounter to Him. I give Him my writing assignments (as if they were mine to give!), and I give Him my leisure. By my surrender of my husband and children to God, I remind myself that they are His anyway; as I yield my problems to Him, I give Him the space to solve them. I have learned that He loves my family and cares more for my work than I do. He is holding all of us and all of our pathways in the palm of His hand.

I enclose the day in parentheses of surrender; in the morning, I ask Him to be Lord of the day, to keep me abiding, and then I claim the assurance that He will do it. I ask Him to bring about what He chooses and to aid me in letting His love flow through me. In the evening, I ask Him to correct my mistakes, to bring good out of my efforts, and I give myself and my loved ones to Him for protection. When I am worried or anxious about a loved one, I abandon that one to His care.

As I lean into the fullness of life, with its complexities and ambiguities, I can yield my will to God moment by moment within the flow of a day's events. As I give up the rights to myself, I am enabled, through a gift of grace, to wait on the Lord's timing. And though I am the essence of impatience and impulsiveness, I am learning to pause throughout the day to affirm the Sovereignty of God and my submission to that Sovereignty. Not only that, but I am even learning to cultivate an attitude of watchful waiting, of relaxed receptivity.

Why then am I surprised that yielding my will "works?" I've heard testimonies of sincere Christians who let loose the power of

God by letting go of the need to control, to be in charge, to be god. And why do I avoid what I *know* will bring me the peace of God? Francois Fénelon has the answer:

> Cannot you see that it is mere folly to be afraid of giving yourself too entirely to God? It merely means that you are afraid of being too happy, of accepting His will in all things too heartily, of bearing your inevitable trials too bravely, of finding too much rest in His love, and of sitting too loosely to the worldly passions which make you miserable.[7]

I am reminded of the mother of Christ, who, when confronted with a most preposterous proposition, chose to surrender her will, her body, indeed, her reputation, to the Holy Other and to participate with God in unleashing divine power.

I am reminded of Christ who anguished in the Garden over the imminent crucifixion but was able to say, "Thy will be done!" I have avoided surrender before because I feared that it would lead me to suffering; I forget, too easily, that Christ overcame the cross and grave to live victoriously and that in surrender to His purpose, I give Him permission to let loose that same power in me. I see that power in Paul, who was determined to wipe out Christians. Blinded on his way to Damascus, he came finally to affirm, "I can do all things through *Christ* which strengtheneth me" (Philippians 4:13, KJV, emphasis mine).

That power and energy is not something I conjure up nor that I manipulate. It is released through me when I allow myself to become His channel. In the powerful old book *Letting God Help You*, John A. U. Redhead says, "I can because he can and because through him I am able. And the source of that power is unmistakable: It is God, who has come close in Christ."

Through the wrestlings of these last fifteen years, I have walked into a new assurance, and through the pain of my own doing, I have begun to learn obedience. I have come to the affirmation that God is very near all the time and everywhere.

On the battlefields of the war I fought with God over who would control my life, I have learned that not only does God expect my surrender, but that He accomplishes, accepts, and maintains that surrender. I cannot do that on my own, and so He must. Only Christ can deliver me of my self-will, and as He does, life is lived according to His intent and plan. I walk into victory, claiming and demonstrating faith over fear, love over hate, and productivity over wasted time and energy. Yielded to God, I have the strength to live my days as a child of God, created in His image with the capacity to love, to be creative and communicative, and to make choices. Under the direction of God, I am empowered to choose life and make small, moment by moment changes in habits and patterns.

The beauty of this life is that I often do not know when I am being carried into wholeness by my choices or through events until I look back over the past. In retrospect, I see how God gave me what I needed to rise above self-defeating choices and make life-affirming ones; I see how He has begun moving me away from a victim stance to the victorious life in Christ. He takes even the setbacks and relapses into old ways and uses them to show me a better way of demonstrating His peace, love, and joy.

As that battle of my will versus God's is resolved, His Spirit is freed to work. As I offer more and more of myself to Him, He is able to accomplish His work through me.

"For it is God who works in you to will and to act according to his good purpose" (Philippians 2:13, NIV).

Meditation has led me to the conviction that I belong to God. He owns the universe and He owns me, and I am His instrument for this time in His universe. When I forget that divine order and return to my state of willfulness, out-of-sync events—those times of disorder and confusion, misunderstanding and strife—will get my attention. When I willingly choose to let this order be, I am then free to live in all its fullness. He helps things come together in a natural kind of harmony, if only I am willing to let Him rule time and space . . . and me.

My strong will can work to the good of God's creation as it is brought under the Lordship of Christ. In the ongoing battles of my willfulness, I have found God to be constant in His activity, and I have come, more and more, to accept His sovereignty. That sovereignty enables me to rest, trusting Him to keep me faithful. I am no longer quite so easily tossed about by life's events and am able to say with Paul: "I am convinced that neither death nor life, neither angels nor demons, neither the present nor the future, nor any powers, neither height nor depth nor anything else in all creation, will be able to separate us from the love of God that is in Christ Jesus our Lord" (Romans 8:38–40, NIV).

In friendship with God, I come to accept that God has His own plans for His kingdom and that my task is to wait until He reveals His will for my part in His design. I empty my heart and mind of my own willfulness and allow His agenda to take over.

That willingness of submission to the only Authority allows the Holy Spirit and the yielded one to work together creatively in a holy partnership. Then it is possible to receive the joy of God's blessings, *however He decides to give them.* Whatever God designs, He will maintain and prosper.

EXERCISE

Begin your meditation time by relaxing each part of your body.

As you inhale, repeat to yourself, "I am resting in God," and as you exhale say, "and I am at peace."

After a few moments of repeating this affirmation, allow yourself to become aware of any tightness in your body. Where are you "holding on" to energy? What part of your body is rigid or stiff?

What part of your life are you still clinging to for security?

What person are you trying to change?

Is there a part of yourself that you have not accepted?

Is there a situation or person you cannot tolerate?

These areas of pain are your growing edges. They are the places where God can do His work.

See yourself confessing your resistance to God. See Him give you the power to let go.

Hear Him tell you that His will is perfection and love and grace.

How will you be different if you let go of your willfulness and let God take charge of this growing edge?

WALKING IN THE LIGHT

"When we inject the truth into our every thought,
taking a therapeutic broom and sweeping away
the lies and beliefs which have enslaved us,
we find our lives radically changed for the happier better."
—William Backus, Marie Chapian

"This is the message we have heard from him
and declare to you:
God is light; in him there is no darkness at all.
If we claim to have fellowship with him yet walk
in the darkness,
we lie and do not live by the truth.
But if we walk in the light,
as he is in the light, we have fellowship with one another,
and the blood of Jesus, his Son, purifies us from every sin.
If we claim to be without sin, we deceive ourselves
and the truth is not in us.
If we confess our sins, he is faithful and just
and will forgive us our sins and purify us
from all unrighteousness.
If we claim we have not sinned, we make him
out to be a liar
and his word has no place in our lives."
—1 John 1:5–10, NIV

71

"Listen to this!" I chortled, propping my feet up on the dash of
our station wagon. Then I read my husband another passage from
Scott Peck's bestseller, *People of the Lie.*

We were winding our way southward through the lovely hills of
Missouri, heading home from the conflict-ridden annual conven-
tion of our denomination. Each chapter in Peck's book on evil gave
me more fodder; I was looking for all the evidence I could find to
nail those "evil ones" who held the opposite position from mine.

"I'd be careful calling other people evil," Martus said quietly,
letting a handful of peanuts slide into his Coke. "It's pretty easy to
label others as evil and miss it in yourself."

He's right much of the time, but not always. This time, I cast an
impatient look in his direction and decided to keep the pearls to
myself. If he wouldn't play "Aren't they awful?" with me, it
wouldn't be any fun. Nevertheless, his admonition tucked itself
away in my mind and heart to be a leveler in my attitudes, and the
powerful book on evil, which I thought I could use to bludgeon
others, became a warning signal for my own life.

What is true for the individual usually billows out into society.
It's pretty common these days to mount attacks on evil at the
drop of a hat; we like to decide quickly who wears the black hat.
It's so easy to assume, once I've had an "awakening," that I am
"into" truth, and when that truth I treasure is questioned and put
to the test, it's easy to cast stones and accusations of "evil" at my
"oppressor." It's too easy to designate a scapegoat, whether it's in
our personal relationships or world relationships; if one can carry
the blame, the rest can go free. Often, I would rather have a hero
or a scapegoat than grapple with the real issues.

The real question for me has to do with the evil in my own life,
and as I have moved deeper into communion with the Truth, I
find myself increasingly uncomfortable with the lies and distortions, myths and games of my daily existence. I have come to see
that part of the meaning of salvation is in the progressive revelation of truth and untruth in the activities and transactions of life
at home, in the marketplace, and in the church. As that truth is
released, my creativity is set free.

When each of us is very young, we make decisions about life. Because children are wonderful observers but terrible interpreters, many of those decisions are based on limited data or on distorted perceptions.

In those early, formative years, we decide if we are safe in the world and if we are lovable or not. We decide if people can be trusted or if we can make good decisions, affect change, make it on our own.

Early on, belief systems evolve about death and dying, money, sex and power, gender roles, racial and religious characteristics, and the right to freedom, success, speech, and love.

Some of these beliefs are accurate and serve us well. Unfortunately, many of our early beliefs and decisions are based on lies, myths, or fantasies. Some of us build an entire life on these foundations of sand. We then build up thick walls of defenses, shutting ourselves off from God and other people. Sadly, the process of building and sustaining these defenses requires huge amounts of energy and blocks the flow of creativity.

As my experiences of encounter with God began to increase, the Spirit of Truth began exposing my distorted belief system. At the same time, I began to have the courage to tell myself the truth about various parts of my life; I realized that I was an expert at self-deception, not because I was a bad person, but either because I didn't know any better or because facing the truth was painful.

Some of the distortions and lies I have confronted in my meditation are quite seductive. They have lured me into trouble, always promising an easy road, but yielding up, in fact, pain and tribulation. For example:

- I deserve good things.
- Life should be easy.
- Someone else is responsible for my problems.
- My work is not as important as my husband's.
- If I don't recognize the problem, it doesn't exist.

- I can live any way I choose.

- If I love you enough, I can make you OK.

- If I try hard enough, and am good enough, God will protect me and give me good things.

- There is a perfect place . . . marriage . . . friend.

About simpler things, too, I have fallen into self-deceptive traps.

- If no one sees me eat this, it won't make me fat.

- I can do this; if no one knows, it won't hurt.

- What I do isn't really important.

The problem with these distortions of truth is that they affect my obedience and right-living at very basic levels, and when I am unfaithful with the most basic parts of life, I am likely to be unfaithful in the big things.

As I began to explore these crippling beliefs, I found that I resisted recovery because it was scary to be whole. That discovery led me to the awesome awareness that avoiding or denying the truth is an instrument of death—to a person, a relationship, a family, or a nation.

So, part of the work of Christ in my meditation was to expose the self-deceptions and, therefore, the evil, which was defeating me so that He could perform His healing. With His Spirit working in me, I was freed to let myself know the truth. As I continue to meditate on Christ, He exposes lies, reveals truth, and then enables me to live out that truth.

As I dwell in the secret place of the Most High, I find that my ability to maintain falsehood begins to crumble. I have, in placing myself in friendship with Christ, volunteered to let Him lead me into truth. So far, He has upset every part of my life, turning over each stone in my wall of defenses and removing the self-protecting masks—all to lead me into truth. He has tampered with my use of time, my career choices, and my self perceptions in ruthless, relentless purging.

* * *

So what do truth and meditation have to do with each other? Everything.

When I am blocked in meditation, it may signal a new era of growth. Since God's Spirit leads me to seek union with Himself in order to change constricting, harmful beliefs, He may be prompting a fresh start or a new direction. I may need to weed out a lie and face truth; I may be at the point of moving into greater creativity and community as I see my life with the clearer eyes that time with Christ brings about.

Sometimes I lean into that friendship because I may have come to the end of my ability and strength and know of no other place to turn. I may have wandered out of the fold: the very desire to return home is evidence that God is coming after me to reveal the truth about myself, my choices, my lifestyle, and my associations.

And when I begin to feel that "mere existing isn't good enough," it is usually a sign that God is using my circumstances to draw me closer to Him. If this is happening to you—if something in you is echoing a dissatisfaction, a "divine discontent"—be assured that in your restlessness is the Voice of God calling you to higher places. It's time to shed the next constricting layer.

We are made for growth and change. Just as plants grow toward the light, we, too, are to turn toward the Light for growth. Unfortunately, there is no way to come into the presence of the Holy One without encountering our own sin (which is why so many of us avoid prayer and meditation!). There is no way to a union with the Perfect One without having the gaping holes of our imperfection revealed. Encountering the One who is righteous exposes my frailties and foibles, my sins of attitude and action, my growing edges. His probing light makes its way into the darkest corners; He seeks and finds me when I try to hide. God is always at work in us, restoring us to His original design, and the discomfort or pain of life has within it the seed of renewal, the possibility of transformation.

Luke 5 offers us encouragement in the story of Simon, who had been fishing unsuccessfully all night. Jesus saw his plight and encouraged him to cast his net into the deep water. Although Simon protested ("It won't work. You don't understand, Jesus. We've already tried that!"), he went along with the Master's suggestion. Luke records that Simon had to call in other fishermen to contain the bounty of fish!

When I am stuck, spinning my wheels, or lost is not the time to give up my discipline, but rather it is the time to go still deeper in the friendship with Christ. At times, going deeper involves gaining new insight or working through some barrier. I make it a practice to "check in" with a pastoral counselor on a regular basis just as I see my physician for a yearly check-up. Once after a six-week period of working on a problem area, the counselor and I were bringing closure to our sessions.

"I'll be back," I said, not wanting him to think I was "finished."

"Oh, I know you will," he laughed. "You'll come in the next time you need to shed another layer."

And so it has been; God leads me to deeper knowledge through meditation, and my counselors help me through the birth process to newness of life. They help me see truth and then stand with me as I implement the new truth. That's the way it's supposed to be when you're walking with the One who says, "I am making all things new." As the kingdom within grows, new arrangements must be made, and anyone knows that remodeling can be a messy, trying project. Indeed, letting go of old habits and prejudices comes hard, particularly when they have become so comfortable. Growth is painful, unsettling, and downright scary.

However, Jesus Christ does not want His children for whom He gave His life to settle for mediocrity or brokenness. His intent is perfection, and so the one who practices Christian meditation can expect a shaking of his or her foundations.

Walking in the Light, which produces growth and change, is painful because there is also a taking on of new habits, attitudes, and thought patterns. Even though I may be mentally convinced of the worth of the change, I may resist it. I may try every easy way that I can think of to avoid change. I can deny the need, try to shift it on to someone else, and look for ways to sabotage the growth, but if I maintain fellowship with the Spirit of Truth, I will soon become sick of myself and look for the next train to the Father's house!

Growth is painful because it requires the exercise of personal responsibility, not only in the big areas of life, but in the everyday, menial events. In this era of equality and liberation, I have been disgustingly dependent on my husband. When I married, I elevated the role of wife above my personhood, and I have often tried to make him responsible for my happiness. Because I have realized that my dependency has thwarted my spiritual growth and our marital happiness, I have been trying desperately to assert my freedom and meet him on the same level, adult-to-adult. My efforts at breaking free have jarred the structure of our marriage, and for the last year or so we have been up in the air, trying to chart some new courses. Taking responsibility for myself and my gifts has been part of the painful process of learning to walk in the Light.

Recently in preparing for a trip, I "forgot" to cash a check. So Martus offered to cash one for me. But in the rush to get off, I left without getting the money from him.

Miles down the road, I realized my penniless plight and was furious with his neglect. That night, long-distance, I chided him petulantly, "You didn't give me my money!"

He sighed—audibly. "It's true you didn't get your money, but you could have remembered it, too!"

Only later could I laugh at myself. I so want to assess faults to others and escape responsibility for my own growth and freedom! The lie I have had to confront is that someone else is responsible for me, someone else is supposed to take care of me, make me happy, and take the blame for my unhappiness.

As I persevere in being transformed to God's image in meditation, I catch glimpses of His desire and purpose for me in open and closed doors, in the opportunities that exist within each problem and through inspiration from others' lives. His dream for me starts feeding into my awareness bit by bit, and I begin yearning to shake the shackles that keep me from living out His dream. As He gives Himself to me in the silence, I hear new calls; then I squirm and chafe until I allow Him to push back the limits I have lived with and fill in the spaces with the flow of His purpose.

This process of becoming new leads us to the truth about ourselves and about God. It exposes all that is false and flimsy to God's refining love and establishes God's truth as the standard against which to measure our beliefs, actions, and experiences.

Walking in the light also moves me from theory to reality, from thinking about God to allowing His presence to work in the everyday events of life and relationships. For years, I have written curriculum and magazine material for youth. I've been in the position of giving advice to adults working with teenagers, but now that I have teenagers, I find that it's not as easy as I thought! Their growth and development necessitates my own changing; their evolution into adulthood is a testing ground for my faith.

I can also expound at length on the theory of the "dark night of the soul." I can hold out a hand of friendship through comforting words and a loving, sensitive presence to a friend whose faith is being stretched to the outermost limits, and I can help that friend see where God is at work.

However, when I am in the darkness, I find the platitudes about "being tested" most unpalatable. What I want is relief, not growth! Don't talk to me about "healing at the deepest level" when I'm hurting; give me a Band-Aid or an Alka-Seltzer fast!

Deep down, I know that this "dark night of the soul" is often necessary. Part of the process of transformation is recovering parts of myself that have been lost. Because I lean more naturally to the intuitive, feeling, aesthetic strengths of right-brain thinking, I have thought that I was a dummy in logical, orderly matters. I knew I was creative in right-brain ways, but God has led me to develop and experience left-brain creativity as well. In that recovery, I am becoming more whole, more balanced.

Through the painful realization that not everyone liked my

spontaneous, off-the-wall approach to life, I've learned to be more reserved, more tactful (but only when necessary!). Through the exploration of my inner self, I have retrieved a childlike sense of wonder; I have increased my capacity to feel.

I am learning though that God's ways are not my ways, but He is most assuredly efficient, using my broken dreams, thwarted efforts, and mistakes to carve a better vessel to hold His life.

Growth is invisible, so I must not be obsessed with "how I'm doing" in my inner life. Instead, I must surrender it all to God, focus on the Risen Christ, and determine to walk a new way.

Another work of the transformation process that occurs in meditation is a moving away from negative, dead-end thinking. Affirm that He is creating a new heart in you, and then try to relax with the process. Try to rest in the assurance that He is at work, one day at a time, bringing good out of evil and order out of chaos.

As God begins to convict you of the necessity of change in a particular area, you may want Him to do all the work for you. He is always able to work a miracle, but He has the audacity to expect us to do our part. Once we've been given the light of knowing what to change, we lose that light unless we act on the knowledge! Acting is the faith lived out.

One of the helpful tools for making changes is affirmation. *An affirmation is a positive statement that you want to be true.* As you yield this process to God, He will direct you to reasonable, attainable, and health-producing affirmations which are consistent with His plan for you.

Basic affirmations relating to the spiritual journey help condition my mind. There have been times when the affirmation "I am a child of God, created in His image" has grounded me in the midst of conflicting expectations. "I am loved and forgiven by God" has created an attitude of grace. "God is with me," or "Emmanuel," enables me to remember I am always in His presence.

Other affirmations, such as "I can create peace" and "I see through the eyes of love," prompt desired, but difficult, actions.

Affirmations such as the following cover the simple parts of life (which are often the most difficult):

- I eat only what is good for me.

- I exercise every day.

- I am becoming more consistent with my daily meditation.

Affirmations may latch on to dreams, helping to bring about a desired good. For instance, to overcome my writer's block about this book, I used affirmations about freedom and completion.

- I write with ease and abandon.

- Ideas come to me quickly and logically.

- I am finding creative silence.

I picture success in my endeavors and use affirmations to condition my mind and heart.

- I am writing well.

- My writing is useful to many people.

Sometimes, however, my feelings want to contradict what I am affirming about myself.

"But I don't feel loving," I wailed when trying to incorporate a loving and gentle spirit through the use of affirmations. "Is this phony or hypocritical?" I wondered. My quest for truth seemed at odds with what I was attempting to create with my inner talking.

It is important, therefore, to recognize the difference between the affirmation and the feeling about the affirmation in order to understand how your own resistance to wholeness or success may work against you. Offer to God that gap between what is true and what you want to be true. Ask Him to close the space so that all of your energies will be focused in the same direction. You *will* be talking to yourself; you might as well be in charge of what you say to yourself!

Because I know too well that my motives are never completely self-less, I have learned to offer my affirmations to God before I make them part of my thought patterns. "As a man thinketh" (and talketh and walketh) is an unyielding principle.

To determine if the affirmations are consistent with the will of God, I ask myself the following questions about them:

1. Does my affirmation violate any of God's laws?
2. Will the result I am seeking harm anyone?
3. Will the result promote the kingdom of God in my life or in the life of anyone else?

As I meditate, allowing God's light to reveal my darkness, I find I need the experience of confession. Because the traditions in the part of God's church where I worship do not provide for confession, I must usually seek it out. That means that confession is outside my routine unless I make it happen; it is an inconvenient, time-consuming ordeal which I avoid until I am incapacitated by my failure to do so. Yet, once I take the plunge, I always wonder why I waited so long to feel better.

And I've noticed, too, that as I seek God in the silence, I am always guided to the place where I can make confession. God always provides the right person to hear my confession and to speak the word of forgiveness, though it may not be the one person I would have expected. He *always* provides the mid-wives for the birth into new life. And though I'm not where I'm going to be in that birth process, thank God, I'm not where I was. Because I am encountering the living Christ, debris is being cleared away, and the channel is being unplugged so that I can let the love flow from God through me out into the world.

> "And I will ask the Father, and he will give you another Counselor to be with you forever—the Spirit of truth. The world cannot accept him, because it neither sees him nor knows him. But you know him, for he lives with you and will be in you." [John 14:16–17, NIV]

> But when he, the Spirit of truth, comes, he will guide you into all truth. [John 16:13, NIV]

Father,
I abandon myself into your hands;
do with me what you will.
Whatever you may do, I thank you:
I am ready for all; I accept all.
Let only your will be done in me,
and in all your creatures.
I wish no more than this, O Lord.

Into your hands, I commend my soul;
I offer it to you with all
the love of my heart,
for I love you, Lord,
and so need to give myself,
to surrender myself into your hands
without reserve
and with boundless confidence,
For you are my Father.

—PRAYER OF ABANDONMENT
(Charles de Foucauld's personalized
translation of the "Our Father")

EXERCISE

After you have "centered" down, using deep breathing and pic-
turing Christ within you, abandon this time to Christ's care. Use
the prayer of abandonment, the Lord's Prayer, the Jesus Prayer, or
any other prayer you choose.

Picture yourself in a dimly lit cell with many locks on the large,
metal door. Each of the locks has a name inscribed on it; the name
represents something or someone you are allowing to bind you.

Visualize each lock, one at a time.

Allow yourself a few moments to feel the trapped, hemmed in,
choked feeling of oppression.

Then, imagine that Christ Himself comes to your cell with the keys to unlock the door.

How do you feel?

Picture Christ unlocking each lock. As He does, He says to you, "I'm freeing you from _____," and He throws away each lock and key into outer space where they disintegrate.

Hear Him say to you, "You are no longer a prisoner. You are changed from darkness into light."

See yourself leaving the cell and walking into a lush garden with Christ. What will you do now?

FREE TO LIVE . . .
FREE TO GROW

"So if the Son sets you free, you will be free indeed."
—John 8:36, NIV

"It is for freedom that Christ has set us free.
Stand firm, then, and not let yourselves
be burdened again by a yoke of slavery."
—Galatians 5:1, NIV

"Now the Lord is the Spirit,
and where the Spirit of the Lord is, there is freedom."
—2 Corinthians 3:17, NIV

"Dance with God;
but be sure to let Him lead."
—W. Norman Cooper

"I want to venture out, but I'm afraid . . ." I moaned to seven
faithful friends at the Pastoral Care and Counseling Center. We'd
been meeting together on a regular basis for nearly a year, explor-
ing spiritual growth issues and helping each other become whole.
Suddenly, all seven pairs of eyes turned on me, and I wished I'd
never opened my mouth! I had the distinct impression that my
breakthrough moment was about to come in the form of a direct,
penetrating confrontation.

"When are you going to quit blaming other people for your lack of freedom?" one voice demanded.

"Isn't it about time you acted on the things you *know* to be true?" another chimed in.

"I don't think you want to be free," the leader of the group challenged. "You keep coming back to the same point of saying you *can't*. It's time to put actions to your words!"

"Yeah, you're the one who talks about walking the walk instead of talking the talk!"

One of the group put the kicker in as a last chorus. "If you choose to stay where you are," she chided, "you can at least have the honesty to admit that you're doing it to yourself."

Stunned, I could clearly see myself at a crossroads. Shaking and close to tears, I knew the adventurous philosophy which I had espoused in my weekly newspaper column, "Growing Edges," was on the line. If I wanted "to walk on the water," I was going to have "to get out of the boat!"

Even in my meditation time, scriptures about freedom kept coming to my attention. What was God trying to tell me? Where was He leading me? And then I remembered that a few weeks earlier my spiritual director had prayed the strangest prayer about me. She had asked God to grant me the *courage* to have the *freedom* to be who He had created me to be. (I'd been a little miffed at her prayer, I remember.)

For years, I'd heard the freedom words of scripture ring in my head. Now it was time to see if I really could live out that freedom He was most assuredly calling me to. I had surrendered my will to Him, and now that decision was to be worked out in reality.

But I didn't fully understand the nature of that freedom. Was it freedom to be exercised now—the freedom to make choices, to be responsible, to express my creativity, to think my own thoughts, and to own my own opinions—or was it a gift of life after death?

As I thought about it, it made no sense to me that God would provide gifts of His abundance in heaven and expect us to live as slaves in this life any more than it makes sense for an earthly father to store up treasures for his children's futures and let them want in the present! The more I knew of Christ through my growing friendship with Him, the more I squirmed under my inner shackles.

Up to this point in my life, I had thought it was enough to be free *from* old shackles. I had thought I'd "worked through" the unhealthy dependencies and distorted ways of seeing. Little did I know that I was on my way to freedom *to* live in the knowledge of God's delight. That freedom isn't license to do anything I want to do. It isn't irresponsibility, and it's not necessarily autonomy.

Why do I say I want freedom, but then fight it, fleeing true freedom by enslaving myself to other persons and to things? I know when I *don't* have it, just as surely as I know what it is to relax *after* I have tensed a muscle.

In the quiet of meditation on the life of Christ, the pray-er inevitably will begin to chafe under the straps of bondage as the Great Liberator does His work. As I sat with my friends that fateful day, I could see that in meditation, I was being set free in new ways to release new forms and depths of creativity. Frankly, I wasn't sure I wanted it. The responsibility for taking risks, making choices, and venturing out in my work and in relationships that went along with the freedom to do what I wanted to do and what I loved was awesome to me.

What I do with this freedom that I have been given through Christ affects the quality of my life and the effectiveness of my service, and so the Christian inevitably comes face to face with the awesome, awful gift of freedom.

Deep within I could hear the echo of Madeleine L'Engle's voice as she had quoted Hebrews 10:31 at a retreat I once attended: "It is a terrifying thing to fall into the hands of the living God" (WILLIAMS). Maybe *this* freedom was part of what the writer of Hebrews meant!

As I left the Pastoral Care and Counseling Center that day, I remembered an earlier warm spring evening, just after Mother's Day, when I was trying out my new three-speed bicycle. It had been years since I had been on a bicycle, and I was a little unsure of myself. Besides, this bike could go so much faster than the one-speed of my childhood.

Faster and faster I went, balancing tenuously on the narrow seat that seemed so high above the ground. The wind was crisp against my face; my legs were churning rapidly. What joy! What freedom! *But what if I were to fall while traveling at this exhilarating speed?* Both the question and the answer flashed across my mind simultaneously.

Suddenly, I stopped dead-still in the middle of the street. I was terrified of my new acquisition; I should have gotten a one-speed. I wasn't meant for such fun!

So it is with freedom. Too many of us fear the life-giving freedom of Christ. (What if we make a mistake?) So in any number of ways, we box ourselves in. We deprive ourselves of freedom by all sorts of good and bad things; we are trapped by our excessive rules for pure living as well as our sorry, harmful habits. We fear success, too, for it carries with it responsibility.

* * *

As I continued to reflect on what my friends at the Counseling Center had said, I recalled a question which was tossed my way by an impudent counselor only days before. "How is it that you manage to find something to feel guilty about in every situation?"

It was a probing question which I immediately denied, and yet the tense set to my jaw and my nervous laughter betrayed my suspicion that the questioner had stumbled onto something. I couldn't be *that* bad, I reasoned; after all, I was enlightened and aware! What had happened to me? . . .

At the first of the year, my spiritual director, my guide and teacher in spiritual growth, gave me a big red book published by Overeaters Anonymous. As I began to read it, embarrassed and ashamed that I even *had* to read it, the veil was lifted, and I saw that "feeling bad" about myself had become a habit. I had turned God's gracious gift of food, which He intended for His creatures' nourishment and pleasure, into a warfare. In an on-going battle with food, I had entrapped myself in the rules and restrictions of dieting, the popular pastime of our era, and had set up, subconsciously, a way to keep myself punished. The misuse of food had become the way I kept myself in bondage.

It seemed to me, as I began to reflect on the confrontations that had come in rapid succession, that God was up to something. Too many people were harping on the same theme. Too many echoes of the same theme were cropping up to call it "coincidental." As I gathered up the courage to look still deeper, I discovered that my bent toward legalism and self-punishment permeated other areas, such as my use of time and money, my acts of friendship and loving. Instead of enjoying my family, I was fretting over them, worrying about their welfare, coming down on them with rules and regulations . . . and what I was called to do was love them!

Even the giftedness which I had discovered had become an awful taskmaster. I accepted too many writing assignments, spread myself too thin with speaking engagements, expecting too much too soon and too often. Once I got myself trapped, I could continue the cycle of punishment and self-pity. "I should not have . . ." or "I should have . . ." took turns with, "You'd better . . ." or "You ought to . . ." in my inner talking. In keeping myself constricted and always "in a bind," I couldn't possibly live out the freedom I had been granted in Christ. Of course, I felt guilty about that, too. The more I sought refuge in God's presence, the more I yearned to be free.

The only area of my life untouched by this perfectionism and legalism was my worship and meditation, and for that I reach back far into my childhood and gratefully thank my parents who never forced a ritualistic approach to God. Because of that early encounter with God, I was able to see my own lack of inner freedom (when it was pointed out to me!); because of the growing intimacy with the Son, who had, after all, set me free, I was able to accept the freedom of Christ and to begin to make some changes in my lifestyle. It was through my early periods of meditation that the work of Christ's Spirit was loosening the shackles of slavery.

Through meditation and the abrasive help of God's "messengers," I was beginning to see the freedom of discipline. It must release me to affirm life, to love freely and elaborately. I saw that I was to live as a free person, as a channel of grace, mercy and justice in the world where God had placed me.

Sometimes gently and sometimes abruptly, God began to transform my attitudes of dread and duty. In my meditation time, I began to picture myself receiving the freedom of complete forgiveness, and I began training myself to notice when I am about to lock myself up again in one of my familiar traps. God is teaching me to observe and correct instead of judge.

As I carry the desire for freedom, I am learning to call on Him, to remind myself again and again that I was not created for bondage, but for abundant, creative living. This is a new, tender, sensitive growing edge for me; the thought of greater freedom is scary to me; but I know it is the work of Christ within me. It is the dying to my old self and the beginning of the new self, the life in Christ.

It is clear to me now that the choice is always mine. I cannot be bound to anything unless I agree to be imprisoned. No one else can make me feel guilty; I volunteer. My freedom does not depend on anyone else; I cannot blame any other human being if I choose to be dependent or bound. If something or someone has indeed oppressed me, then I am responsible, once I become aware of it, to allow Christ to break the chains. To remain in bondage to food, drugs or alcohol, sex, pleasure, work or family is to fashion idols of destruction. To allow myself to be bound by my own fears, guilt, or hatred is nothing short of sin.

Indeed, as I become conformed to the image of Christ through union with Him, I will even be freed to forgive my oppressor. I will let go of things which tie me in knots and defeat me; I will take the gifts of God and use them instead of being mastered by them.

Meditation, then, or union with Christ, is the way I put my will in safekeeping. It is the harbor for my leanings toward self-punishment and self-destruction. It is there, in the receiving of God's grace, that I give up my attachment to the false gods of the world and yield my allegiance and worship to God in Christ. Maintaining that conscious contact with the Supreme Being protects me from attachment to lesser gods.

Meditation keeps me "in my Father's house," safe and protected from the Evil One. As I pray, I am grounded and centered, no longer tossed about and victimized by my own fears and compulsions. I am freed from my propensity toward darkness. Meditation gives me the courage to live creatively instead of destructively.

The model of this freedom is Christ. He was totally free from internal as well as external oppression because He knew who He was and what He was about. Most importantly, though, Christ was free because He was totally obedient to the Father, and that obedience was nurtured as He drew away to the mountainside or to the lake for communion with the Father. He knew He must abide in the Father; Jesus drew His very life from His Father, and so He was free.

One day, as I was sitting with my spiritual confidant, I began to let her see the depth of my self-punishment, the despair of my bondage.

"How will you begin to claim the freedom of Christ?" she asked. She always wants *specifics.*

I began to stutter out some ways I could change my behavior.

"But I'm afraid I'll go too far," I wailed. The very thought of freedom scared me to death.

She began to laugh riotously. Self-consciously and shyly, I tried to join in, but I failed to see the humor. I knew, somehow, that the joke was on me!

"There's no danger, Jeanie. It will take you years to shake the habits of legalism. Don't worry about going too far!"

I had to laugh, too, but then I sat quiet again, deep in thought. The warm fire crackled; snow fell gently in the evening twilight.

"Legalism can be just as deadly as libertinism," I whispered softly, aware for the first time how tragic it would be to live out an entire lifetime, following all the rules but never living out the gaiety of grace. How sad to remain a Pharisee and never know the life-affirming celebration of being a true disciple of Christ.

What can I do, then, to make sure my freedom is His freedom and not my willfulness? I can study and meditate on the life of Christ and see how He lived out His freedom. By asking Him to teach me to dance to life instead of living as if I were in a funeral march, I can affirm the fact that the Cross was enough. I don't need another Calvary.

And so, I write my own Emancipation Proclamation.

Freedom in Christ means that, under His Lordship, I can give love and receive it.
I am free to accept the gifts that He is eager to give.
I am free to affirm the gifts of others and to enjoy them.
I am free to trust that He really will never leave me or forsake me.
I am free to live guilt-free, hate-free, fear-free; to open my hand in trust to the world.
I am free to use my gifts in loving service.
I am free to accept that which I cannot change.
I am free to hope.
I am free to be victorious instead of victimized.
I am free to accept another just as he is because I am accepted and loved just as I am.
I am free from unhealthy dependencies.
I am free from the sovereignty and rule of other people who do not love me as much as God does.
I am free from twisted thinking and irrational, unrealistic expectations. I am free to make new decisions, based on current data.
I am free from the need to rebel, to force my own will, to control the destinies of others, to change what is not mine to change.
I am free from striving and fighting—I am free from fear.
And I am free to play, joyfully at home in the universe of my Father.

How much time and effort I will save myself if I follow the model of Our Lord! How much grief and sadness I will avoid if I would detach myself from lesser gods and attach myself to Christ. How much more abundant my life will be if I will live out the truth of John 15 in the everyday affairs!

I must not, however, despair, feeling guilty because I haven't done it all perfectly up to this point. The task, I must remember, is that I am "on the way toward becoming perfect." The challenge is to move toward the Light, assured that He will meet me at the point of my need. He will empower me to seek freedom from that which is not worthy of my worship, as well as allow me the grace of freedom *in* His Spirit.

It is possible to break free of whatever thwarts the kingdom's growth. It is possible to overcome whatever keeps you from union with Christ. Once you have caught a glimmer of this freedom,

have felt it in your whole body, you will then be able to pass it on
to someone near you who needs to hear the Good News.

I sat again with my friend, months after her probing inquiry into
my talent for feeling bad.

"You're different, Jeanie. You're not angry anymore," she said.

Startled, I let the warmth of her words drift down like gentle
petals around my awareness.

"What's happened?" she asked. "You're much freer."

"I think that in the darkness of the past year, I had the rug
pulled out from under me. I saw many of the things that I valued
threatened. I found out that I had to give up my dependency on
others, and so I found God in the cloud. Then I learned I could
be who God created me to be." (My words came spontaneously,
but their full import continues to be revealed.)

"And you got free there, too, didn't you?" she asked, and
added, "This is just a shadow of things to come."

EXERCISE

As you enter the quietness, picture yourself standing before a
judge. You've likely been in this courtroom before; you are what
they call a "repeat offender."

This time, however, the Judge is Christ and His "sentence" is
"Freedom!" Listen to His voice.

"Go and sin no more."

"Nor do I condemn you."

"Live as a free man."

"I have come to set you free."

As you sit in the silence, hear the jury agreeing with Christ.
You turn and look into their faces, and you see loved ones,
friends. You also see yourself there, too, seated with the jury.

Hear each one pronounce the sentence of grace and mercy.

How do you accept the verdict? As a gift or as a curse? If they
aren't going to condemn you, will you?

Shift your attention and imagination to the Cross.

Hear the words of Scripture: "For God so loved the world that he gave his one and only Son, that whoever believes in him shall not perish but have eternal life" (John 3:16, NIV).

Open your hands and your heart to accept this complete forgiveness.

Live in freedom for this moment. As you live in this grace-filled moment, you will be able to live the next moment in grace, also.

C·h·a·p·t·e·r N·i·n·e

A SLOW AND CERTAIN LIGHT

"We can all see God in exceptional things,
but it requires the culture of spiritual discipline to see
God in every detail.
Never allow that the haphazard is anything less than
God's appointed order,
and be ready to discover the Divine designs anywhere."
—Oswald Chambers

"And the Lord will continually guide you, . . ."
—Isaiah 58:11, NASB

"Trust in the Lord with all your heart
and do not lean on your own understanding.
In all your ways acknowledge him
and he will make your paths straight."
—Proverbs 3:5–6, NIV

It was after midnight and long past time to go home. For several hours, friends and I had been problem-solving and praying, and out of the evening had come a solution to a long-term problem of mine. Their idea surpassed any I had ever imagined and opened up possibilities I had not even known how to consider.

As I left their home, I was charged with energy and inspiration. It all seemed so right. Hope and excitement filled me so that it seemed the day was just beginning. I knew that trying to sleep would be a waste of time, even at that hour.

Quietly, I made my way in the darkness to my car. Suddenly, birdsong pierced the night air with a brilliant, clear song. I stopped, caught by the appropriateness of the moment's melody; what is usually morningsong ushered in a new era for me. God's purpose and guidance had been at work, even when I couldn't see ahead of me.

That moment is vivid in my memory, but so is the difficult and perilous journey that had led to that moment of God's breaking through the darkness of my searching and struggling with His specific and clear direction.

For months, I had been seeking guidance. I had made some big decisions and was now at the point of needing to take the next step. I knew it was time to take a new direction when I began waking up in the middle of the night with the cold sweats and a pounding heart. In my heart, I cried out, "I'll do whatever you want, if I can just *know* what it is you want!"

Fear had me in its icy grip. I questioned previous decisions about vocation and direction related to my work, which had seemed so right at the time. I chastised myself for making those decisions, for it seemed that, even though they had opened doors of ministry and service, perhaps I had been premature or hasty in my actions.

Confusion reigned right alongside the fear, and the more I kept turning backward to judge previous decisions, the more I was gripped with fear about the future. Caught in the vise between past and future, my present was anything but Spirit-filled! Vacillating between too much action and not enough, I was as effective as a car spinning wildly on ice, going nowhere good, fast.

Finally, I began pulling myself up out of my darkness, fully aware that confusion and fear are not productive tools for dealing with problems and challenges. Taking myself in hand, I made my way back to my spiritual confidant and began seeking God's plan for the next stage of my journey. Once again I was taking those important three steps: I can't do it. He can. And I'm going to let Him.

My friend led me to a deep study of the Song of Solomon, a study which held a terrific surprise for me. I had never spent much

time there, but as I read Watchman Nee's exposition of this powerful book, I began to see that my inability to receive God's guidance
was directly related to my belief system. I was a stingy receiver of
God's direction and His blessings because I was so good at making
it on my own—until now. Finally, I had created a problem over
which I was powerless, and only God could restore stability, balance, and serenity.

As I drew closer to God during this period, I had no idea how
He was going to lead me, but I believed with all of my heart that He
would. I did not ask Him to release me from my situation, but to
give me the guidance, direction, and resources to work it out.

In the weeks that followed the surrender, I found that the most
difficult part was walking the tightrope between taking responsibility for my part and letting go and letting God work. Knowing
when to wait and when to act, separating what was God's business from what was mine was a constant challenge.

Through the weeks of searching and waiting, of struggling with
the questions and the insecurities, I began to realize that He was
leading me still deeper in fellowship through this specific phase of
my life. Following His instruction to the disciples to "cast their
nets on the other side of the boat," I went deeper into His Word
and deeper into my meditation than ever before, and I cast my
attention in other directions, too, seeking guidance and instruction among new friends and through new thought processes.
Later, I was to see how perfectly He worked in the guidance.

As I tuned in to His work, I became especially sensitive—I
lived on tiptoe, *expecting* to receive His guidance. I had asked Him
some questions, and I took time to listen. I prayed in order to
know His will, and I worked at hearing.

Periodically, I reviewed God's leading in my past. I would recall
how He had made rough places smooth and had rolled away stones,
even when I wasn't aware of His activity. Sadly, I also recalled those
times when I had lived oblivious to His activity and on my own
power, but then I would affirm His forgiveness of those times of
waywardness.

During that period of living out on the raw edge of faith, I
reaffirmed my desire to be God's instrument of reconciliation and

grace. I recommitted my gifts to Him, giving Him permission to lead me to use those within His divine plan and purpose . . . and that scared me to death.

"I know God doesn't lead you to a place only to dash you off a cliff," my mother said long-distance, and that word came at a time when I was holding on by my fingertips. "He's guided you all along," she said, "and He's not going to quit now."

And, so, the God of time and space led me to that spring-night marathon with my friends to show me His purpose through the suggestions and collective wisdom of fellow seekers. As my friends spoke, each adding an idea here and there, I began to see that God had been at work all along. Why was I so surprised?

In my search for God's guidance, I began to see that at the root of my fear was the belief that maybe this time God would turn His head. Perhaps He'd given me the grace and guidance before, but because of my willfulness, this time He would withhold it! Perhaps I'd gotten the signals wrong before, and it was all catching up with me! Perhaps He was going to punish me. . . . All of those fears and misperceptions about who God is and how He works were dark and thick cloud layers, blocking His love and guidance.

Through those months of stretching my faith, I began to return to the simple, childlike response of obedience and trust. God does guide His children, and He does act specifically; living out of a centered faith through a life stance of prayer opens me up to receive the guidance. It's simple, but it's not easy.

It would be so much easier if harmful and evil things didn't sometimes entice me into thinking they were good for me. Those times when no answer is easy or good are painful. To discern what is the best is sometimes so confusing that it is easier to settle for what is good. To choose between two equally desirable routes is hard because it means I must, in saying yes also say no.

I am tempted, when caught in the dilemmas of choices and challenges, to march around demanding God to show me where He is! Instead of drawing near to Him in prayer and waiting in expectant receptivity, I tend to take charge, seize control, and begin to do *something*, even if it's wrong. My omnipresent willfulness supersedes the willing omniscience of God.

In the very midst of every difficulty, God is at work drawing us closer to Him, and so the key to managing these decision times is in drawing near to God, knowing that the light of His guidance will certainly appear. *The key is to enter into meditation, not in order to solve problems, but to find God.* That encounter will provide you with all the resources you need to make the necessary decisions and choices.

Allowing God the rule and reign of your inner kingdom is evidence of obedience, and all through Scripture it is clear that God never failed to provide guidance for those who were willing to obey. It is His intent and His pleasure to guide and to give His children what they need to do the job at hand.

Maintaining the daily discipline of union with Christ will eventually nurture a Christ-consciousness. As you become familiar with His nature and character through Scripture, worship, and the shared life of Christian community, you will learn what He expects and desires. As you know Christ, you will know His will.

So it will be with the guidance of God. As your knowledge of Him grows, you will not have to debate the "ought-ness" of certain routes; you will be developing an internal standard of measurement.

The challenge, as you grow in maturity, will be in maintaining the willingness to obey and the courage to follow His guidance These abilities, too, will grow as you allow God to strengthen you in meditation. As you allow Him to fill you with His resources, you will gain courage to live in the wider plane of His grace.

*   *   *

So what if I've been faithful to the disciplines of the Christian life? I have sought and even encountered the living Christ in my meditation, and I still have the problem! Things are *still* unsolved. What am I to do?

Guidance *will* come, and so the challenge is to carry the assurance of God's presence, that inner knowing, into the midst of your daily activities. All through the Scriptures, there is direction about the need for constancy in prayer. See Luke 18:1–8 for Jesus' humorous direction for persistence, and gain strength from Ephesians 6:18, Isaiah 55:6, and 1 Chronicles 16:10-11.

In moving toward living under God's guidance, I start and stop, advance and retreat, slip and slide—depending, regretfully, on the intensity of my need. However, I am learning that constancy in my meditation leads to constancy in seeing His guidance. His guidance is present all the time as a sure and certain light. My receiver needs constant adjustment, it seems, but that is the function of communion with Him.

I have poured over Isaiah in the middle of long, aching nights. I have perused the Psalms, underlining, memorizing, and repeating the promises of God to His people. In the silence, I have pressed the promises in my memory, training my mind, and now I am finding that these Scriptures bubble up into my consciousness as I go about my activities. The seemingly spontaneous reminders of God's presence, the momentary arrest of my thoughts to focus on the only Reality that counts, give me the boost of stamina I need to make it to the next phase. *God can be trusted to keep me abiding throughout the challenges and questions of the day.*

When I am stymied, I ask God to reveal any ways I might be blocking His purpose. Often, in the stillness of meditating, I remember something I decided I didn't want to do. There was someone I chose not to forgive, an act of love I decided was too much trouble. Perhaps I had wasted time or money; I may have turned away from a seeking child or a hurting friend. Sometimes I choose not to act on inspiration for an article, or I just simply let other responsibilities and demands crowd in on the time I had been given to write. As I let go of whatever it is that is hindering God's guidance and activity, a space in which His will can move is created.

I also block God's guidance by my fear of success. As I look back on my life, I see how I slowed down God's purpose because of a fear of "making it." This tendency shows up best as I look at my habits of procrastination; I tend to come right up to the completion of a project and never quite finish it. This falling short of the mark cripples God's purpose. It is almost as if I have been afraid of God's blessings, and I can see now that my awareness of that tendency is a result of God's guidance.

Another way I avoid or reject God's guidance is my persistent refusal to see God as He is. His way is perfect, and yet I fear that I won't like it. The reality is that there is indeed suffering in life and the way of the Cross does propel us down avenues that stretch and strain, but the presence of God in the midst of life is the key to victory—a victorious journey made possible when we surrender our wills to God and allow His presence to have priority.

I also block God's guidance as I go after answers and provisions first and His presence as an afterthought. I demand His presents and refuse His presence! The condition for receiving His direction, then, is always seeking first His presence and His rule. If that is a habit instead of frantic one-shots in times of trouble, receiving His guidance will be perpetual.

Finally, I block God's guidance when I don't take action. Refusing to make a plan and begin moving forward when it is time keeps me in a state of stewing and struggling, whereas timely action somehow helps the process along. Meditation coupled with action carries and creates energy and genius, and doors begin to open seemingly effortlessly. I don't know how it happens, but I know that it does!

If I choose to extinguish the light I have been given by refusing to act on what guidance I do have, I set in motion the possibility of returning to darkness. If I don't act on the guidance I have been given, God will look elsewhere for a willing servant. If I refuse to obey what I *know*, confusion and uncertainty are bound to descend into my affairs!

Perhaps God has given me direction and I am *willing* to follow Him, but my *want-er* won't cooperate. I don't want what it seems that He wants. I don't even want to want His will! In the quietness, and as I seek union with God, He will bring these points of resistance to my awareness. He will forgive my rebellion, neglect, or carelessness. He will usher me back into the light.

When that resistance to God becomes so painful that I finally recognize it as rebellion, I realize my need for confession and repentance. In the quietness, I surrender my desires to Him and ask Him to bring my heart into conformity with His will. I don't force my feelings to change, but focus simply and trustingly on His power. As my friendship with Him grows, a slow and certain change will evolve. I will begin to recognize more of His loveliness so that what is lost will be nothing in comparison to what is gained by His life growing and flourishing in me.

For me, the "streams in the desert" of God's guidance have come in specific ways, but it takes the ability to see them to know that it is God at work. I am given the ability to wait or to act, and in either, God somehow provides the patience for waiting or the courage for leaping into what appears to be darkness.

God gives guidance through His people. He reveals direction through impressions, images that seem to come out of the blue. Guidance may come unexpectedly from a conversation with a friend and "a word fitly spoken." As I am seeking to live under God's rule, consistency of Bible study breaks open His instruction. I become aware of divine synchronicity; direction comes at the right time and is confirmed in specific ways.

God sometimes works in what appears, at first, to be strange ways. Often, I don't see His fingerprints until later (and that makes me wonder what other messages I have missed!). Sometimes God even works through strangers.

Three years ago, I accepted a job with a parenting organization to develop and lead a program of education and support for parents of young children. I had the qualifications and the training for the job. I had community contacts as well as interest in the field.

This was something I could enjoy doing, and it fit—sort of— with what I perceived to be my call. Besides, I felt I needed to supplement the family income, and since this was a part-time job, I felt I could balance it with other responsibilities. It seemed right.

From the beginning, disaster reigned. As time wore on, I wore out. And it became increasingly clear that I had made the wrong decision. Being a die-hard, though, I held on, trying to force it to work. All of my energy was depleted in solving problems and confronting crises. There was nothing left of me for doing what I loved, to fulfill the call I had discovered and defined. In short, I was miserable and was making everyone else miserable.

On a cloudy, dreary February morning, as I was dealing with the job, my telephone rang. Wearily, I moved to answer it, expecting still another problem from my job.

"You don't know me," the young woman began and my heart sank. I didn't *want* to know anyone else.

"I was in your Sunday school class one Sunday about a year ago. Could you please talk to me sometime today?"

There really wasn't time that day, but for some reason I set an appointment with this young woman, and she came to talk over, of all things, her despair with her job and a yearning to move out into a field which she felt would enable her to express her strengths and gifts.

When I came to myself, I heard my own voice urging her to do what was right for her, and to move out away from what kept her imprisoned. I heard myself encouraging her to have faith in her gifts, to risk by choosing excellence and quality.

Only after she left and I was alone in the silence of my darkened house did the thunderbolt hit. "You sent her here for me! That speech I made was for my benefit, not hers!"—I thought I heard God laugh out loud. Every time I think of that young woman, I remember that God still sends His messengers to His children if only we can have the grace to recognize them when they come.

*   *   *

When I am waiting on the Lord, it is important that I do more than simply sit and wait for Him to act. Once I have surrendered the questions and choices to God and asked Him for guidance, it is important to go on about my business or, as Oswald Chambers says, to do the next thing. The point is to keep that center of stillness, that internal waiting on God, while going ahead with life.

Instead of putting my energy and effort on hold, waiting for that flash of lightning or insight, I can take care of my immediate responsibilities. If inspiration is lagging, I can throw myself into my duties. Sometimes God breaks into the midst of the most mundane chores to open a window.

Many times I have worked long and hard on a writing assignment, only to hit a hard spot I couldn't seem to conquer. I know
intimately the dreaded dearth of writer's block when nothing
"comes" to me. On one early spring day, I was stuck. So, disgusted
and discouraged, I shoved the papers aside and went outside.
Since spring was beginning to hint at its arrival, I took the shovel
and began to turn over dirt in the garden area. As I relaxed and
took my mind off the problem, guidance was freed to bubble up
into my awareness. I was able to return, again inspired, and complete my assignment. I have repeated that experience on numerous occasions.

When seeking guidance, then, it is important to look to God
instead of at the dilemma. Pray to Him instead of to the problem.
Instead of focusing your attention on the problem, thereby creating what you don't want, focus on God and His provision. As
you commit your efforts to Him, wait in relaxed receptivity for
Him to guide.

As you give yourself to God and allow Him to work in you, He
will open and deepen your awareness. You will know without
knowing *how* you know. You will have insight and understanding that you cannot prove or document. You will become able to
distinguish His guidance from that of others, and you will make
leaps over logical steps to come to conclusions through intuitive
knowing.

Intuitive knowing has not been valued or encouraged in our
logical, materialistic society which relies on hard data and proof.
Eastern cultures elevate inner knowing above rational knowing,
but Western culture discounts intuition.

Things are changing, however. With the research into whole-
brain thinking and with the growing evidence of the consequences
of our materialistic philosophy in business, the nuclear arms race,
and medicine, people are beginning to accept what artists have
always known. What appears on the surface to be right or true or
best may not necessarily be so.

Trying to document intuitive knowing in a world that demands
logical explanation is frustrating. However, allowing Christ to work
through both parts of the mind, learning to listen to those who are

left-brain creative, and to act on both logical and intuitive leading releases the ability and courage to act on what cannot be proven.

The safeguard for me is always in community with other believers. I need the faithful counsel of other sincere seekers. I need their honesty to correct me when I go too far in risking and their encouragement when I am afraid of going further. I need for them to tell me when I'm full of baloney or if I'm about to fall off a cliff. I need the correction of those who are serious about abiding and obeying. I need the collective wisdom and the shared life of Christ to sustain me in my journey.

The air is thin, out on a limb, and the ground is far away. On one winter day two years ago, quivering with fear at the prospect of venturing out to still another challenge, I made my way to seek guidance from a faithful friend. She helped me identify my fear, my excuse to avoid the work I *knew* I had been called to do. She confronted my excuses and stripped them away to expose the refusal to cooperate with God.

But then, after all of that, she said, "Next week, while you're busy doing the work, I will have faith for you. I will carry that so you can be freed to work with abandon." I need the slow and certain light that comes in the midst of community.

The gift of knowing, when you don't know how you know, is the gift of discernment. It is inspiration. It is guidance. But, it is all of that *only* as it springs out of a deep, abiding relationship with Christ. It is a gift only when it is infused with the Love of God and paired with the willingness to obey. It is a gift which must be received with awe and reverence.

Finally, while waiting on the Lord, it is important to maintain a joyful attitude. Being joyful doesn't mean that we must deny the pain, rather it is a recognition that God is present in the suffering. Fretting and complaining only clog the lines of God's directions and keep us hobbled in moving forward. Being joyful doesn't imply a giddy, false kind of pretense at victory, but a clear, secure confidence that God is in charge. It is His world, and you are His child. God doesn't require us to *feel* joyful; the command is to rejoice. We don't have to *feel* grateful; we are just implored to give thanks.

God can handle our feelings. He can handle any outpouring of honest feelings. What He wants is not for me to wallow in feelings nor to worship them, but to look beyond my feelings and circumstances to His provision and His presence.

In meditation, I am given the grace to rest, secure in the knowledge that if I have the presence of God, He will provide all that I need in order to follow even what seems to be the hardest guidance.

As I obey and follow the Light, I will be given guidance as surely as the day follows night.

If you really believe in God, He will put it all right. God is willing and able by His Holy Spirit. Stop expecting the solution from yourself, or the answer from anything there is in man, and simply yield yourself completely to God to work in you. He will do it all for you.[8]

EXERCISE

After you have centered yourself in the presence of God, abandoning yourself to Him for this time, focus on the image of God reaching out to you.

Do not ask anything of Him; concentrate only on His coming to you.

Repeat silently "I receive Your Spirit" or "I receive Your Life." (Note: This is different from imploring Him to "be with" you. We do not need to ask or cajole God into being with us; He is always here. What we must do is train ourselves to know He is here, to become so accustomed to His nearness that we know we have found the place where we are never alone.)

Feel God's presence all around you. Imagine Him even in your heart. Hear Him say, "It is the Father's good pleasure . . ."

If a problem or decision comes to you, let it linger only long enough to give it to God's safekeeping. Then return to focusing on God's presence within you.

You are here now, in this present moment.

You are to leave the past to God's mercy.

You are to place the future in God's care.

Be fully present here, now, in the love of God.

Bringing our desires before God, we will discover if they are from Him or our own illusions.

Time will tell.

Meditation is not a push-button proposition; God is not an errand boy. Meditation does, however, cultivate the soil so that we can receive the guidance.

We forget to make room for God to come in as He chooses. . . . Do not look for God to come in any particular way, but *look for Him.* That is the way to make room for Him. Expect Him to come, but do not expect Him in a certain way. . . . Keep your life in its contact with God that His surprising power may break out on the right hand and on the left. Always be in a state of expectancy for God to come in as He likes.

—Oswald Chambers

$C \cdot h \cdot a \cdot p \cdot t \cdot e \cdot r \quad T \cdot e \cdot n$

LET THE LOVE FLOW

"I believe . . . not only do self love and love of others
go hand in hand, but that ultimately
they are indistinguishable."
—Scott Peck

"Meeting God in other human beings
is the most costly part of the dialogue between
God and man."
—John Powell

"No one has beheld God at any time; if we love one another,
God abides in us, and His love is perfected in us."
—1 John 4:12, NASB

It had been one of those days. Everywhere I had gone, love had demanded a listening ear, a consoling word, a patient heart, and frankly, I was worn out! All I wanted to do was change into my walking shoes and pound out my fatigue on my well-worn route through neighborhood streets.

The January wind was cold as I rounded the corner and headed out on my three-mile trek. I plunged my hands into the pockets of my windbreaker and from one pulled out the frayed devotional book I used on these walks. My eyes stung from the cold, but I focused them on the words of guidance for the day. This was to be my refueling for the rest of the day's challenges.

"Pray for others," it said, and I silently screamed. "I've been taking care of everyone else all day. What about me? Who cares about praying for me?"

I stormed down the streets, rehashing all the giving I had done that day. From an early morning doctor's appointment to an afternoon stint in the hairdresser's chair, I had listened to grief and crisis. Everyone I met, it seemed, had had a problem with life, and I had silently drawn on God's power and love all day. But now I wanted somebody to love me! It was my turn.

Somehow, I pulled my attention back to the rest of the devotional thoughts, deciding I would go ahead and give it a chance. I took a deep breath and started in, praying first for my loved ones.

Suddenly, a different Spirit took over my prayer. As if outside my control, I began to pray for the people along my walking route in the houses where I knew the dwellers. There was the home where a new baby was expected . . . the place where close friends lived . . . the family who had a runaway child . . . the blended family, where each member was trying to find a place . . . the home where my children's best friends lived . . . the house where I had experienced rejection.

As the prayer seemed to pray itself, I found myself asking God to bless each one who came to my mind. On and on I walked, praying house by house, block by block, and as I placed the focus on others, my fatigue evaporated, and my spirits began to soar. My feet were light now, and I was filled with the wonder of God's love for myself and for all His children.

Returning home, I was refreshed and restored, ready to participate in love with family and friends. Christ's presence had given me love so that I could pass it on. My energy had returned, and I was able to let the love of Christ flow unhindered. What a privilege, I marveled, to pray for others and to love them for God.

In order to fulfill our potential as we walk in God's story, I believe we've got to understand that there is a kind of energy, a kind of power, available to us as Christians that people in the left-brain, logical world do not understand. That power is released not only by prayer, but also (primarily) by loving.[9]

That process of being refilled with love and energy has happened many times since I began receiving God's love in meditation. He has guided me to specific ways of loving and has given me the grace to love at particularly difficult times. He has also exposed my inability to love in specific and sometimes embarrassing ways. I am learning that to enter into love is to walk into the refining fire . . . and that fire is hot. To enter into love is to open myself up to an ongoing cauterization of the ego.

Being loved by God sounds like a great idea. In theory, I was all for it. I had certainly experienced and heard about the love of God all of my life. However, for some sinister reason, I had a habit of focusing on the judgment and wrath of God more than on His love, and when I began to experience that love through daily meditation, it upset my status quo. Oddly, I clung to my fear patterns and habits, holding on to their comfort instead of giving in to the freedom of living in God's story of love and acceptance. And, so, God had to begin the process of breaking down my resistance to His love in order to make a space for His love to exist.

I didn't consciously choose to oust God's love; perhaps I was afraid of it. Perhaps I have been afraid of feeling too much joy or freedom. Maybe my sense of unworthiness was deeper than I ever realized; sometimes I held on to my bad feelings and self-recrimination as if there were safety in them. Through it all, however, His love continued to pursue me. He wanted me to experience His love so that I could pass it on to others, even when my responses were unloving.

* * *

"I can always tell when you get up early for your quiet time," my husband said. "You always chew us out at breakfast!"

What an indictment these painful words were to me. How I longed for them not to be true, and yet it seemed that what he said *was* true. The contrast between the quietness of my early morning meditation and the noise of the family's preparations for the day was so jolting that I had difficulty making the transition.

My husband's comment about my early morning behavior brought me to some new self-knowledge and spurred me to some needed changes in my daily habits. He also helped me see that if what I was experiencing in my quiet time was not yet real and if I couldn't live the love out in the family crucible, then I hadn't really learned it. Somehow, I was blocking God's love. Again and again, it is back to the drawing board—and my prayer closet—with my selfish, willful nature.

At other times when I would be away on a prayer retreat, there was always a stressful time coming home. Often, arguments and accusations would explode within the first twenty-four hours. It was as if I could get that vertical relationship with God worked out, but the horizontal ones with friends and family members were too much. I *wanted* to love my family as God loved them, and I wanted to be more patient and tender; why was it I was such a bear at breakfast?

Surely, as I became more responsive to God's love, I would be magically freed of broken relationships and could love freely. Surely, love would flow unhindered once I had my meditation practices refined. I fully expected God to reward my seeking with smoothed-out relationships and a conflict-free home life. After all, I was trying to love and be loved. . . .

As I began to experience God's love in my times of meditation, however, other forces seemed to be doing battle with the horizontal part of my life. There would be moments when the intensity of loving God and loving others would be overwhelming, and I knew I could translate the feelings into actions.

Then, perhaps in the same day, I would experience the brokenness of relationships. The contrast between the prayer experience and the living out of love was excruciatingly painful. I was experiencing the painful cauterization of my lifelong self-centeredness.

Since I am inherently a relational person, I had always prided myself on my ability to love and be loved, and yet I was puzzled by recurring difficulties of the same nature with significant others. I was plagued by something—now I know it was a deep fear—that held me back in closeness or in risking. I had many friendships, but it became clear that God had some lovework to do in my closest relationships.

As I stayed with the meditation that focused on receiving God's love, He did me the favor of showing me how I had confused pleasing others with loving them. I had worked like crazy all of my life to get others' approval, all the time thinking I was loving them. I had given what I needed, trying to fill up the space of insecurity and loneliness, and when my fervent efforts didn't produce the kind of response or result I wanted, I became angry.

It wasn't that I was always selfish or that I couldn't get along with others at all. Nor was it that I was a complete cripple in love. It was more that my ability to receive and give love had some strings attached that kept it bound. There was a lack of freedom in love. Instinctively, I knew there was something more.

I moved around the vicious triangle, alternately playing the roles of victim, rescuer, and persecutor, all of the time thinking that I was the one who could love and others couldn't! I was a classic co-dependent: my self-worth and ability to love were enmeshed in others' approval of me.

Gradually, I began to see that there was nothing I could do to make God love me any more or any less; His love was unconditional at any given moment. I branched out in that awareness with the same kind of care and caution I used in testing the waters of a lake. Bit by loving bit, however, He began freeing me to accept that love and then to start giving it to others. The blocked love began to thaw, and where I had tried to get love, always with the result of creating conflict, I began to give it.

I began to see that my loving others was cramped by my fear of others' disapproval or rejection and that I hid my fear behind all sorts of adaptive and reactive behaviors. Out of my fear, I had formed the habit of dependence, thinking I was loving. I would go along, seething inside, all the time becoming more and more alienated from myself and from others.

As I let God love me through creative visualization and meditation on Christ's love for others in the Gospels, I began the process of letting go of fear and branching out in loving courageously. I became willing to meet people straight across, without the need to put the other person up or down, and to be vulnerable enough to reveal my feelings and thoughts. I became more honest and was able to lay down some of the fig leaves of protectiveness. I became willing to be seen just as I was, a little bit at a time.

As I relaxed into God's love, I felt the healing process of self-acceptance and self-respect grow. No longer did I have to pretend that I wasn't strong or creative or fearful or angry. I could allow myself the full range of human experience, and that self-acceptance freed joy and love to flow through me to others.

Whereas I had allowed others to set my agenda, plan my time, and define my worth, I began to let God's love be my standard. Suddenly, I saw how others had preempted God's sovereignty and had become idols. As my boundaries of selfhood became more firm, I loved more freely and abundantly. No longer did I rush in to rescue someone else so that I would have a place. I accepted my place in God's design and set others free to be whom God had created them to be.

Loving is indeed a process, and growing edges continually emerge that need the tender care of God's corrective love. Through prayer, I become sensitive to how I block the loveflow; through prayer, I receive the courage to move out of my brokenness to love others with God's love.

To live in the presence of Love was to become aware of all the ways my loving was inadequate and to accept His way of loving. To receive God's love was to know the reality of love that casts out fear, and since fear had been my most common emotion, there was sure to be a backlash of resistance. Entering into the depths of Christ's love was to expose all the ways in which I was keeping love from flowing through me to others. Little did I know that the decision to love God was a decision to change my way of loving others. To choose love is to choose change, for love always precipitates a crisis.

Prayer, then, became God's loving corrective, and I began to see that love—the kind that led Christ to Calvary—was going to cost me more than I had planned on paying. I had thought I would enter into this new relationship with God and others and encounter no risks. The risk was that I would have to lay down my familiar protectiveness and defensiveness and learn to give in new ways. Indeed, He would give me a new heart by giving me a new vision.

What I would be learning, for the rest of my life, is that my vertical relationship with God is intimately bound to my horizontal relationships with family and friends, neighbors and strangers. And while I, a proponent of modern psychology, had tried to get to God by fixing up my earthly relationships, He would show me that I must reverse that order. As I could receive His love, I would grow in my loving of others. Contemplative prayer that focused on Jesus' kind of loving would revolutionize my relationships, starting with my relationship with myself.

The recognition of the directing of the flow of love is crucial. In union with Christ, I *receive* His love; then in obedience to His command, I love. My resources, which God has graciously loaned to me—my gifts, time, money, energy, insight, etc.—are granted to me not for my enjoyment, although enjoying them is not *wrong*. These gifts are mine to use in loving. The important task is to see myself as a channel through which God intends to love the world, beginning with those closest to me.

The reality is that we must live together, and to survive, we must learn to love. God and I aren't a majority, as some would flippantly taunt; God and I are in community with believers and pilgrims and backsliders and doubters around the earth. No Christian lives in isolation, and the very fact of claiming His lordship brings me face to face with the need of a broken, hurting world for the Love that is capable of healing the wounds. If I am called into relationship with Christ, and if I am going to claim the name of "Christian," then I am called to love and to love beyond the boundaries of what is comfortable. Often, I am called to a love that stretches my heart beyond my understanding or my endurance.

So, then, meditation and the ensuing friendship with Christ lead me to confrontation with my need to love and others' need to receive it. At the same time, that practicing of the presence of God as a regular discipline is the way I receive the freedom and grace to love creatively.

What do I do, however, when I feel unloved and unwanted? Sometimes, I experience "all this love I have to give" as a huge stick of dynamite, just waiting for some lucky receiver. At other times, the love relationships I'm already in are so distorted with conflict and misunderstanding that I'm not sure it's worth it. There are those awful times when my love is spurned or misunderstood and no matter how I lavish it, it is rejected.

When the Evil One is really on a roll with me, I question the reality of love; if loving is so hard, it must not be real. My love sometimes seems to make so little difference, I want to withdraw it. That condition leads me straightaway into the acknowledgment of my selfish love, of loving others to get them to love me, and of co-dependency—that distorted, dependent substitute for real, honest, free love.

If I decide that love is too hard or if I refuse to love, I am choosing to die. If I stop the flow out of fear or selfishness, I will become sick and afflicted. When I allow hate and apathy to choke out love, then I can expect to be miserable and lonely.

Whatever I am seeking, then, I must begin to give. I don't understand why that works; I only know it does. I must put my bread upon the water and give love without concern for whether or not it's appreciated or recognized. I cannot afford to be in the black with my loving.

As I meditate and am consistently accountable to my spiritual counselors, I begin to recognize unhealthy patterns of loving. I see how I set myself up to be rejected; the ways I have of defeating love are revealed. I learn how I sabotage relationships with unrealistic expectations, by nonacceptance or dishonesty, by allowing fear to overrule love.

In meditation, I learn how to love the significant others of my life in the specific ways they want to be loved. As I bring each loved one before the Father in the quietness, listening for His word instead of telling Him what to do, He will guide me into the way of loving that is consistent with His character. God will not give me a quick fix or a cheap trick. He won't tell me what to do to change someone else. He is not after superficial healing or now-and-then love; instead, He enables me to accept and appreciate the uniqueness of each loved one.

He turns His cleansing love to reveal any sin that blocks the flow of His love through me. He gives me the grace to forgive, the eyes to see the needs around me, and the strength, if needed, to love with tough love. God shows me how to grant others the same freedom in love that He grants me.

This on-going process of loving has been setting my loved ones free to be who God created them to be. God continually reminds me that it is not mine to control or manipulate my loved ones, that He loves them even more than I do.

As a safeguard to my need to change or control, instead of love, I have begun praying Christ's prayer in John 17:11–17 for my family and friends. Instead of imposing my agenda on these loved ones, I pray that God will make them one with Him, give them His joy, protect them, and make them useful.

In praying this prayer, I am, in essence, agreeing with Christ's prayer, but I am also saying, "I'm willing for You to have Your way with my loved ones. You don't have to do it my way. I'm not even sure I know what is best for them, but I know that You know."

I also pray Paul's prayer in Ephesians 3:14–21 for others. I ask God to strengthen His presence in my loved ones, that they may be rooted and grounded in His love, and that they will know the extent of that love. God can work out the specifics; I simply express my love through Scripture, giving God room to work in His way.

So many helpful tools have come out of modern counseling and psychology. Through these helping professions, we can learn how to help ourselves, improve communication and productivity, and survive the slings and arrows of an outrageous world. With all the good, however, it is necessary to sift out that which is harmful, and one of the most deadly tools of our time has been in the catch-phrase, "I've just got to get my needs met."

Using that philosophy, people have broken up relatively good marriages and torn innocent children's lives into shreds. I have seen individuals abandon jobs, shirk responsibility, and reject the church or a helping group of seekers because "it wasn't meeting my needs."

"Getting my needs met" is a dead end, for I will *never* get all of my needs filled. If I wait until then to start loving, make a commitment, be a contributor to life instead of a sapper, I will live in constant frustration. It is only in giving that I receive; it is in dying to my own needs that they are met.

When I spend time with God, however, I lose the unhealthy and unbalanced compulsion to have my needs met by others. As I yield my needs to Him, believing that He is, in fact, big enough to fill them, I gain the trust to *leave* my needs in His hands. When I close my meditation time, I must say, "I trust you to take care of that need," and then show my trust by reaching out to meet another's need.

In the process of receiving and giving love, nurtured by your daily meditation, you will begin to recognize the love of God in places you never expected. Instead of seeing the disharmony and failures in community, you will see more of the love. Instead of censuring and judging your brothers and sisters, you will move toward accepting, forgiving. You will move away from skepticism and distrust to trust and belief in the goodness of those you encounter. You will begin to celebrate the miracle of the unity of Christ's spirit even in the midst of great diversity.

Just because you are seeking to love, however, doesn't mean that the world will be whitewashed for you. The Evil One stalks his prey, desiring to defeat those who are striving to walk in the light. One of his favorite tools is disharmony and conflict within the body of Christ.

Choosing to love means choosing to risk hurt. When I open myself up to loving, I open up the possibility of suffering. Allowing myself to identify with another evokes strong feelings and vulnerability. Loving is risking rejection; it is agreeing to participate in the suffering of the world. It is moving beyond detachment, that popular form of withdrawing responsibility for another, to entering into the healing of the other in healthy, giving love.

Our church in San Angelo is a new one, and because so many of its members are young, almost every death in the congregation has been sudden, violent, or somehow outside of the natural order of life and death. Deaths seem to come in two's or three's, creating a time of intense giving and nurturing for my husband.

As I have participated with him in the grief ministry, I have been overwhelmed with fatigue because of the energy drain. I have stretched my empathy and walked through awful, unpleasant situations with him. Later, trying to recover my own equilibrium and re-establish order in a household upset by others' crises, I have realized the cost of loving. I have reflected on the One who participated in our suffering, who has borne our grief. I hear His probing question to the disciples: "Can you drink of this cup? Can you enter into the suffering of my creation and be my instrument of grace and love?"

Only by the grace of our Lord can we live up to the calling of love. Only by abiding and obeying can we withstand the awesome joy of loving and being loved.

When you find yourself in an atmosphere where confusion and disharmony reign, you will understand the grief of Christ when His children are ruled by the Prince of Darkness. As you become more sensitive to God's spirit, you will become more sensitive to the places where hate and selfishness, greed and the drive for power reign.

As I took seriously the work of love in my own life, I began to take the Scriptures as my objective standard and guide for loving. I went to the Gospels to see how Jesus loved those whom He encountered, and I was confronted by the Sermon on the Mount. In this discourse, meant for the serious follower of Christ, injunctions for loving are clear and simple, though deeply profound, and I began searching for instruction for loving others with the kind of transforming love that Jesus had when He lived and walked on earth.

It wasn't long before I was confronted with the way Jesus turned the values and practices of loving upside down. What He asked seemed impossible to fit into my society of the "me" philosophy. What was I to do with these hard teachings? Would it be possible to carry on my life with others without judging or without fearing what is to come? What about forgiving? And what about admitting my need by becoming "poor in spirit?" Could the meek really make it in human relationships? How would I ever be secure enough to love with the kind of freedom and openness that Jesus commanded?

As I poured over these teachings, I began to understand that Christ would not have taught this if it were not possible, and so I began to test out what I was reading. I discovered that receiving God's love gave me the courage to love others; again, the flow of love from God to me and out to others became important. I would give acceptance and forgiveness to others in proportion to my ability to receive, and regular encounters with Christ in my growing prayer life increased my ability to live and love out of Christ's standards.

The amazing thing is that letting the love flow unhindered by judgment, defensiveness, attack, and criticism creates what seems to be a prayer made visible. Praying and loving seem to be so intertwined that it would have been difficult to tell where one ends and another begins. And as I give love, forgiveness, and grace, I find that I receive it.

In conflict, I visualize Christ standing between myself and the other person, loving each of us and bringing peace and harmony. When I am "conscious," I can "breathe love" in the midst of fear and misunderstanding. These short mini-prayers of focusing redirect my attention and release my tension so that God's love moves unhindered between us. The result is that I let go even more and let God's love do the work of restoring and healing.

God's presence enables me to claim His love and be willing to let go of failures and resentments. Regardless of what others choose to do, I have discovered that allowing myself to be His instrument of loving in the world and being willing to be a conduit of love makes it possible to enter into the joy of Christ.

The only hope for peace in a family or a church is in the outpouring of God's love. The only chance we have for peace in the world is for each one who is called into relationship with the Prince of Peace to make himself available as a channel of love.

Starting here. Starting now.

EXERCISE

Use the following prayer by St. Francis of Assisi for this time of meditation.

Lord, make me an instrument of Thy peace.
Where there is hatred, let me sow love,
Where there is doubt, faith,
Where there is darkness, light,
And where there is sadness, joy.

O, Divine Master, grant that I may
not so much seek to be consoled, as to console;
to be understood, as to understand;
to be loved, as to love.

For it is in giving that we receive,
it is in pardoning that we are pardoned,
and it is in dying that we are born to eternal life.

Use a journal to record each phrase, internalizing the meaning of each line for you. You may want to center in on one phrase each day, or use a phrase each week.

How is God working to make you a more useful instrument? How is God using you as His "word made flesh" in loving someone else?

What will you have to give up to be God's instrument?

What will you gain?

Allow God to meet you in the silence with His plan for your loving.

C·h·a·p·t·e·r E·l·e·v·e·n

HUMAN INSTRUMENTS

"This is what the church is meant to be in the world.
We live together as a colony of heaven in an
occupied territory.
Our ultimate loyalty, customs, values and quality of life
are not of our culture but of our Lord and His Kingdom.
The church is to be a foretaste of eternal life,
an experience of heaven in miniature."
—Lloyd Ogilvie

"If only they could all see themselves as they really are.
If only we could see each other that way all the time . . .
I suppose the big problem would be that we
would fall down
and worship each other. . . ."
—Thomas Merton

"For we are His workmanship, created in Christ Jesus
for good works,
which God prepared beforehand, that we should
walk in them."
—Ephesians 2:10, NASB

"It would be easy to practice the presence of God if we didn't
have to fool with water sprinklers and disgruntled church members!" I complained to a brilliant West Texas sunset.

My vantage point was the freshly sodded lawn of our church's new educational building. I sat cross-legged in the gathering dusk and watched my husband fiddle with a contrary pipe. "He shouldn't have to do this!" I thought.

Before my whining had a chance to become a litany, I was struck by the almost audible awareness: "This is the very crucible in which you will find me. This is where and how you will learn to love—in the midst of imperfection and frustration, loving and serving my children."

That set me back on my heels and reminded me of my own imperfection and my propensity for wanting to escape the hurts and difficulties of living in community or in family. I had complained loudly and ferociously to my husband as we walked in the summer dusk to the church, leaving a houseful of noisy children. Loving others was hard!

We took a different route going home, and I took another approach. God had broken through my petulance not just to reveal my sin, but to touch me with love, and I could spend the remaining quiet of the last half of our walk reaching out to my worn and weary husband.

God didn't actually *touch* me, but I felt different. He didn't speak out loud from the heavens, but I heard an inner voice calling me to love. I didn't *see* God with my physical eyes, but I saw His creation with new eyes, and with inner seeing, I knew whom I had met. I encountered God in the very midst of the ordinary.

I cannot increase in fellowship with the living Christ, who was the great Lover, without being filled with love, or being confronted with the puny, self-centered quality of my love, and I have discovered that if I love God first, love for others follows. As I express that love in service to my fellow human beings, I am loving God, and the love in my heart grows in action. The action and the feeling feed each other. It takes some doing, however, to work this out in the imperfect world.

* * *

How then shall we live in community as contemplative people? What does the prayer of the heart have to do with the church and my involvement in it? What can I expect from other seekers of this Friendship? What will be required of me?

It would be easier to limit my participation in religious matters to the Christian television services and programs. I can turn them off when they bore me; changing channels might roll up a more interesting speaker or a zippier singer.

The cost of involving myself in the church is great, and the church is so imperfect that I often wonder if it's worth the effort; yet somehow, I am convinced that the church is the very crucible through which Christ intends to accomplish His work.

The contemplative lifestyle sharpens my need for community. What I hear in the darkness of my closet must be confirmed by those who are walking in His light. I must have the back-and-forth dialogue; those who are on the spiritual pilgrimage are essential to my mental health, spiritual growth, and emotional well being.

God has not called most of us to the solitary life, although it is natural and healthy to seek times of solitude. He has called us to participate in the body of Christ, to call on it when we hurt and to be available for another's pain. He has provided in the church the place for discovering and exercising gifts. He wants His church to be the agent of change in the world.

Through the community of faith, God instructs, corrects, tempers, interprets, confronts, comforts, and loves. It is important to participate in the body life to fulfill the mission and ministry of Christ; it is important for me to participate so that my mission and ministry might be nurtured and fulfilled.

My part of this journey of commitment is to take seriously my churchmanship, and that leads me more deeply into meditation. What I perceive in the silence I carry back to community to be confirmed, used, or corrected. What is learned and experienced in dialogue with other believers provides seeds of contemplation. The movement back and forth between solitude and involvement, the inward journey and the outward, is essential for creative living.

To surround yourself with serious seekers is to provide a place of protection. Receiving from their growth, learning from their experiences, is invaluable in facing the challenges of a secular society.

To live counter to the culture; to give when the world says horde; to love and trust when the world says fear, hate, and be suspicious; to forgive when the world says get even is to set one's self up for difficulty. The strength of other believers, whom you know and have allowed to know you, is one of God's ways of taking care of His Children. Fellow Christians, through the interaction that takes place in the church, can bolster each other. The body life of the church equips its members to do the work of Christ on earth and to be that incarnate word in contemporary society.

As meditation deepens my ability to perceive the working of God and to see things more from His point of view, I must inevitably face the realization that I am the Church, be willing to accept it as it is, and then begin to give the qualities I want from it.

One of the Evil One's greatest tricks is to deceive us into thinking that church should be perfect. He wants us to believe that it isn't any good because of all the hypocrites and that if it isn't perfect, we should give up on it. (He uses that same trick of irrational idealism to defeat us in our marriages or in our efforts at creativity.)

There are, scattered here and there, groups of believers who are attempting to live out the model of the New Testament Church. There are churches which are attempting to live the Gospel in the market place, and there are pastors who are sincerely ministering to the people entrusted to their care. There are those places where neither legalism nor secular humanism is taught, but where there is the breaking of the fresh and life-giving Word of God.

None of these churches is perfect. Not all of the people in them are serious seekers after Christ's presence. Nearly every member, too, is a bona fide hypocrite, to lesser or greater degrees. One of these churches may be in your community. In fact, your name may be on the membership list, but you have not recognized the Light that pervades the life of the church.

If you decide to participate fully in the life of a body of believers, commit to Christ and His people so that you will not be tempted to give up when the going gets tough. Live into your commitment as if you are responsible for the well being of the church, allowing Christ to guide you in your meditation as to how that commitment should be demonstrated.

"I can tell you what is the hardest thing in the world to do. Building a faith community is the hardest thing." The words were Gordon Cosby's, one of our retreat leaders, and they came from years of experience. Our retreat group had come many miles and from diverse denominations to what we perceived to be "the model" church, a church that had learned to balance the inward and outward journeys. Yet we saw, as we lived among the members, that the price was great. We also saw that the power of the Light was even greater.

Where do I begin to participate? How do I find a body of believers where I can both give and receive? How do I move beyond unsatisfactory church life and worship to abundance in community? What is to keep me from focusing on "getting my needs met" even in church life instead of yielding myself as broken bread and poured out wine for the sake of another?

To begin, start where you are. Open yourself up in prayer to be available for a deeper sharing with other believers. Examine your own life, laying aside your need to "have your needs met," and then cultivate that air of expectancy. God will provide community for those who sincerely desire it, and He will enhance the quality of shared worship and fellowship.

Like attracts like, and just as those who are sensitive to the voice of Christ hear his voice, those seekers will also find each other. If, in my meditation, I am indeed encountering the Holy Other, then that quickening will attract others of like mind and heart. I hear a phrase or see an expression in a face which lets me know that I have found a friend on the journey. Eventually, as we share in the Life together, I discover that I am no longer alone. There are others who share my journey of bringing my life under His Lordship.

> So then you are no longer strangers and aliens, but you are fellow-citizens with the saints and are of God's household.
> —Ephesians 2:19, NASB

The work of Christ in me in meditation will be radiated as I share my experiences with another hungry beggar. We get to keep the light we have been given only as we light the way for another.

Members of Alcoholics Anonymous have learned this, for they know they must practice the Twelfth Step in order to stay sober. "Having had a spiritual awakening . . . we tried to carry this message to others. . . ." If an alcoholic's sobriety is dependent on sharing the good news of healing, so is my need to share what God is doing in my life.

Meditation will give me the courage to give witness to my journey, for if I keep it up long enough, I will be transformed. I cannot keep the light under a bushel. I will want others to know Christ, and I will find ways to express the Christ-life naturally and in a manner consistent with my personality and my gifts. As I nurture and practice abiding and obeying, God will bring into my life the ones He wants me to love, just as He will provide the guide I need for my own journey. As I agree to be a transmitter of love, He will sharpen my senses to another's pain; often, I spot the pain in another that I have in myself. By witnessing to what I know of God's healing love, both of us find our ways to wholeness.

*   *   *

Carole Hovde, my friend and fellow pilgrim and one of God's instruments of healing and love, understands some of my deepest needs and fears. I know she is in touch with the divine because she always seems to know the right question to ask, the next path to suggest, the next book to give me. The life of Christ in Carole reaches out to fan the flame of my life.

Sandra Hulse, my artist friend who has provided guidance and content to my spiritual search, knows how to confront my lagging creativity, to affirm the purpose and intent of God's working through me. She isn't afraid to peel away my darkness because she has faced her own. She is bold and incisive in her dealings with me, ruthlessly hacking away at all that does not befit a child of God. Through her, Christ speaks to me.

There are others who reveal Christ to me, and as I receive of the Bounty through them, I am learning how to give it. I am learning to see beneath obnoxious behavior to the pain and to extend God's power to the pain. I am getting new eyes to see beneath the masks of inferiority and fear and am learning to bless the real person instead of reacting to the facade. All of that is being made possible because I am receiving God's mercy and grace in the quiet of my inner sanctuary and in the noise of community.

These faithful friends are my church, human instruments placed in my life by design. When I accept the people who are in my daily traffic pattern as God's gifts to me, I am encouraged. Every meeting of persons becomes the possibility for encountering God. We are His instruments and not just seatmates on a trip through time.

I don't understand how God works in drawing near to us through others. It is a mystery to me that He draws us together at all. The flourishing of Christian friendship among people in our broken, hurting society is so revolutionary that I am compelled to acknowledge the hand of God.

That any of us is able, in scattered spaces, to do acts of love in spite of inherent selfishness is miracle indeed. That we can over-come the fear of each other to give to one another, that we can risk rejection by revealing needs and desires, that we can keep on entering into relationships in spite of past sorrows is clear evidence that all is not lost in our society. Christian community, imperfect though it may be, is clear evidence that God is not through with any one of us or with His Church. It is a sign of hope. The fact that we do as well as we do at sharing out of our brokenness astounds and astonishes me. The Friend who is all faithful must be at work, after all.

* * *

Meditation will open you up to amazing possibilities of friend-ship. It is how God carves out the capacity to love. Shared in community, the practice of the presence of God is a treasure of infinite worth. It is one of the ways the kingdom is let loose in the world.

As we pray together, the unity of the Spirit of Christ becomes real, and while it is mysterious and inexplicable in terms of charts and graphs, those who participate in the shared silence and the focusing on Christ's presence are touched by His love in unique and powerful ways.

This silent communion weaves bonds of healing between marriage partners who focus their attention on Christ's presence between them. The common prayer threads moving back and forth in a sickroom hold a powerful effect. The intense sharing of silent prayer allows God to unite friends in strength and compassion. I don't know how it works, but I know it does. When there are no words to express the depth of feeling of the human heart, the Spirit of Christ works in the silence, interceding on our behalf to the Father and from Him to us.

* * *

The song of a bird through an open window and the warmth of shared memories and shared seeking permeate the stillness of a sun-splashed living room. We settle in for our prayer time; catching up and accounting to each other has paved the way for this time of centering in together.

We sit in the silence together, focusing on the Life that makes communion, fellowship, and celebration possible. Together, we abandon ourselves to the Spirit and participate in a growing bond of Christ's life. We focus our minds on a common prayer of affirmation.

Changeless and calm, Deep Mystery,
Ever more deeply, rooted in me.

That inner Knowing, that ancient Mystery, weaves together a union of human instruments. Emmanuel. God is in the midst of us.

Later, I look across the congregation where I worship. Love helps me see each familiar face with acceptance and compassion. As we encourage each other in the life of faith and participate together in acts of ministry, we are practicing the presence of Christ. And we are doing what we can to flesh out the Spirit of Christ in the world, using our individual creativity to express His love.

EXERCISE

In the silence, see your closest family members or friends. They are seated in a circle, and Jesus is sitting among you. You are out of sight.

See Jesus lovingly touch each of your loved ones.

Call Jesus to you. Ask Him to reveal to you how you can love each one.

Call each one by name and then wait in the quiet for Him to tell you how to love each one.

Imagine that He is giving you all you need to love that person.

Picture yourself entering the circle and giving each loved one *exactly* what Christ wants them to have from you.

Anticipate the freedom of healing and love which will flow from Christ's life through you into the lives of others.

You can practice this meditation with one other person. Visualize a broken relationship or a relationship you are trying to nurture. How are your friendships going to be different because of the love Christ gives you in the silence?

C·h·a·p·t·e·r T·w·e·l·v·e

OUT OF THE DARKNESS

"You will have times of spiritual dryness.
It is the Lord's way."
—Jeanne Guyon

"Do not think that I came to bring peace on earth;
I did not come to bring peace, but a sword."
—Matthew 10:34, NASB

"What I tell you in the darkness, speak in the light. . . ."
—Matthew 10:27, NASB

There I was, limping along, holding on by my fingernails, wondering how I had drifted into another far country. I thought I had perceived God's directions, but maybe I hadn't heard Him right.

I thought I had come further than this . . . I thought I had conquered this terrible fear that is gripping me! My growth pains are tearing at me, and I know that the silence of God is evidence that, once again, I am being ushered through another dark night of the soul to a new level of awareness of God's presence.

Those times of drought are allowed by God to expose the parts that are not worthy of the high calling of Christ, and they contain within them hard questions from Christ to me.

"Do you love me?"

"Do you trust me?"

"What do you want me to do for you?"
"Who do you say that I am?"
"What is your name?"
"What are you going to do with me?"
I couldn't believe it! Here I was, after all these years, in a dry
spell. I knew, with my head, that this new phase of questioning
and searching was a natural part of the ebb and flow of spiritual
growth, but my restless heart ached with the silence of God. And
then, in my reading, I stumbled upon voices of another time.
These voices had encountered the darkness, just as I had, and
they spoke hope to me.

. . . God has only one desire. Certainly you can never understand
a dry spell unless you understand what His desire is. His desire is to
give Himself to the soul that really loves Him and to that soul
which earnestly seeks Him. And yet it is true that this God who
desires to give Himself to you will often conceal Himself from
you—from you, the very one who seeks Him.[10]

The silence reveals the question and then yields the strength
and guidance of God to answer the question and live the answer.
It is always part of the process of wholeness and is the way God
moves his sword against the sinful, broken, fearful parts of my life
that need to be excised. My questions made me open to seeking
God at a new level.

God always ignores the present perfection for the ultimate perfection. He is not concerned about making you blessed and happy just
now. He is working out His ultimate perfection all the time 'that
they may be one even as We are.'[11]

Where are you, God?—My struggle didn't end just because I
wanted it over with in short order. It seemed to me that God had
left me and I could not find Him. As I walked about, carrying on
the daily responsibilities, but searching for guidance and battling
my self-will run riot, I carried on the inner dialogue with this God
who seemed to be hiding.

The questioning for me usually falls along the same lines, and at the core of the question is the issue of whether or not I am going to let God run the world. I question the direction I am to take. I wonder if He is going to take care of things and provide. I wrestle with Him as I work through relationships and conflicts, and yet in the struggle, I find Him and new depths of His love.

I screamed silently, yearning for some visible, tangible proof that God was there. I had been looking for Him, searching in churches and in libraries, along city streets and in quiet countrysides. I cried out for evidence of Him in lonely night watches.

I thought, one time weeks ago, that I heard Him in someone's voice and saw Him in a kindly face, but then I decided that surely that was my imagination.

Where are you, God?

Why don't you move through the clouds and show me that you are Real? Do you hear me? Why don't you answer?

The silence of God billows all around me . . .

Slowly, out of the formless void of my inner silence there emerges a Knowing. He *is* there, after all, but a greater thing is that he is *here*, within me, inside me, closer than my breath. I need not yell or beg or cajole any longer. He is here! He is here indeed.

Be still, and know that I am God. [Psalm 46:10, NIV]

* * *

Sounds and smells of dizzy Brazilian streets assault my senses and my travel-weary body. We—Martus and I and a group of friends from the States—run for a bus, trying to stay together as we jostle with the rush-hour crowd. Pushing and shoving, the noisy throng carries us along to the next sputtering bus.

Martus and I leap onto the bus as it pauses briefly for new riders, and as I look back, the doors close before my friends' startled faces, and the streets of Rio de Janeiro rapidly separate us from each other. Uneasiness washes over me as I realize their dilemma: they do not know the language. Foreign sights zoom by the speeding bus, and I feel alone and scared for them.

Suddenly, in the chaos, there is that Presence, and this time it stills my racing heart. Calmed and comforted, my mind clears to make a space for creative problem-solving. I smile at my strap-mate who tries to communicate in her native Portuguese, and I know our friends will find their way back to our beach-front hotel.

Lo, I am with you alway [Matthew 28:20, KJV]. . . . *Do not be afraid* [Matthew 14:27, NASB]. . . . *The earth is the Lord's and all it contains* [Psalm 24:1, NASB]

＊　＊　＊

Four of us from our church sit together, late into the night, silent, and broken by a tangled maze of lies and distortions. Conflict and confusion mingle with the heavy heat of summer night to choke our energies. Angry words spat back and forth now hang between us in awful pauses, carving deeper chasms of separation and alienation.

The ticking clock marks time, and the revolving sprinkler outside grates on raw nerves; would we ever make it through the brokenness to reconciliation? Is it even possible for healing to take place, or will hatred and fear defeat us? My lovely living room, designed for serenity and comfort, barely contains the anguish.

Where had God hidden this time?

And then, a strange, unbidden burst of courage stretches embryonic limbs against my heart. Drawing upon a power I thought was bludgeoned, I deliberately pull myself up and assert that I will live my life as a test case. Love *is* stronger than hate; faith *really* is greater than fear; God *is, in fact, more powerful than the Evil One* . . . and we move toward reconciliation, one step, one conversation, one conflict resolved at a time.

Peace I leave with you; My peace I give to you; not as the world gives, do I give to you. Let not your heart be troubled, nor let it be fearful. [John 14:27, NASB]

* * *

Is it really worth it, trying to live in accord with the inner promptings of God's Spirit, instead of meeting all the expectations of the church, my family, friends, and acquaintances? Shall I use my gifts and develop my creativity? Wouldn't it be easier to do somebody else's call than to live out of my own call and mission?

Maybe I'll just rest for a few months. I've been pretty busy, and I think I deserve some time off. Besides, others need a turn to do good deeds. I would really like to learn how to play tennis . . .

But, I'm not all that happy idling my motor. I'm even bored; life is colorless and flat. It isn't the needs of others that are calling me, and it isn't others' demands and requests that prompt me into action. Somehow, I can't rest. My mind is ablaze with ideas and desires to do and express and create. It is as if some Force greater than I am is providing the impulse; I am propelled by a surge of energy and excitement . . . and I thought I wanted a break.

You did not choose Me, but I chose you, and appointed you, that you should go and bear fruit, and that your fruit should remain, that whatsoever you ask of the Father in My name, He may give it to you. [John 15:16, NASB]

* * *

I know what it's like to run up against a dead end. Closed doors are all too familiar, and I am acquainted with the bitter taste of discouragement. I can make grand starts—in relationships, in projects or in tasks—but then the inspiration gets crushed and tarnished with everyday cares and the crippling bent toward apathy and mediocrity. The dry dust of fatigue chokes the life out of the smallest endeavor.

Where did the vision go? What happened to my enthusiasm? Maybe God wasn't in this after all. If I had known how hard it was going to be, I would never have had the courage to begin . . .

And, then, almost imperceptibly, new life emerges and fresh winds begin to blow. I *can* make it! All I needed was this one sign of encouragement. I just needed one small breakthrough, a glimmer of remembrance and assurance that You are in this with me.

I will open rivers on the bare heights, and springs in the midst of the valleys; I will make the wilderness a pool of water, and the dry land fountains of water. [Isaiah 41:18, NASB]

*　*　*

That dark night of the soul is inevitable. All the contemplative writers speak of the anguish that comes when the presence of God seems to have vanished and only a darkness of confusion and emptiness echoes back to us.

Those times of questioning self and God are bound to occur. Even the most faithful follower of Christ and the most consistent, disciplined pray-er eventually walks into a valley of death.

I would like to have my testing in theory, but the dark night of the soul may be played out in a marriage crisis, a health breakdown, or a career dead end. Traumas with children or broken relationships, financial problems or conflicts with in-laws may be the place where your testing comes. Sometimes the questions come in the area of your greatest strength, and you may doubt your ability, your intellect, or creativity. You may even question your salvation . . . or the Savior.

The reality of the free will is an awesome, awful force. It is a terrible responsibility; how much easier it would be if God had made us puppets.

Since it is so, though, that I am free and my neighbor is free and the alien and the prisoner are free, I must reckon with the possibility of sin. I must force myself to admit the reality of the Evil One.

* * *

It was a hot summer week, and I was living out a dream. I had gone to Creativity Week at Laity Lodge to spend a week with Madeleine L'Engle and to try to break out of my writer's block of self-doubt and confusion. I had anticipated this week for two years, since Sandra Hulse had placed Madeleine L'Engle's *Walking on Water* in my hands, and I had decided I *must* learn from this deeply committed Christian artist.

Once at the camp, however, I had called home and discovered that Amy, my youngest child, had a high fever. I had tossed and turned all night, wallowing in worry and guilt over being away from her. Surely, I would not be permitted the luxury of feeding my mind and soul at the feet of this distinguished writer! Surely, I was being punished for my selfishness. My place was at home, like any good mother's.

After my restless night, a morning call informed me that Amy was only slightly better. Should I go home?

I sought out Suzie Jaynes, my Sunday school teacher from my college days, and frantically related my anxiety and guilt. I told her of the traumas in our church during the past year and how I had found it almost impossible to write.

"The Devil doesn't want you to write," she explained, shocking both of us. Later, she told me that she had never before attributed a specific activity to the Devil. I had avoided talk of the Devil like the plague; it seemed to me that blaming the Devil was an easy out, a convenient way to shrug off personal responsibility. Besides, people who talked too flippantly about the Devil seemed to take fiendish delight in his antics.

Suzie and I prayed together, leaning on the rail overlooking the Frio River, and I decided to remain at the conference. It was then that I began to see the darkness for what it was; I began to see that the extent to which I move toward God is the extent to which the Evil One moves toward me!

Later in the week, as Madeleine L'Engle and the other retreat leader spoke on the dilemma of free will and the Evil One in the creative process, I began to see that, indeed, the Evil One had been taking great delight in my inability to let God's love and creativity flow through me.

The grip of darkness has only recently lifted. I don't believe the Evil One caused it so much as I allowed hate and fear and guilt to grow in my heart. Then it was that the Prince of Darkness gleefully triumphed.

As you journey with God, you can anticipate the dark night and decide ahead of time that you will ride it through to the Light. As you walk into the darkness, determine to allow the wanderings and doubts of the darkness to produce growth.

Even as you struggle in the darkness, claim the assurance that others have traveled this same path and rest in the knowledge that you will finally again encounter God. In the faithfulness, you will show that you can bear a little more of His light; God will meet you even in the darkness. Don't fight the darkness, and don't condemn yourself. Wait on God; He will speak.

In the darkness, learn to be patient with yourself. Affirm "God is at work even now" or "God is here." Condition your mind and heart by repeating "Even now, I trust God will meet me again" or "I trust God with all of my life." Turn to someone who is spiritually mature for guidance and assurance.

Continue to look to God. Keep your disciplines. If it is unbearably painful, take some time off from meditation, vary your approach or use your energies in service. However, the more closely you can keep centered in His presence, the more of Himself He will give to you. Once you have crossed into the Light, you will see His design in allowing the darkness.

As you go about your daily paths, tinker with your problems as little as possible. We increase our distress when we focus on the problem instead of God. Picture yourself giving even your darkness to Him.

When I become unproductive or unloving, I can allow that discomfort or pain to lead me deeper into friendship with the True Vine. If I'm not growing, I've learned that the disciplines of the Christian life are what God uses to water my roots!

Christian meditation will change your life. It will make you more creative, loving, and trusting. It will improve your ability to live with family and in community with others. It will sharpen your awareness and appreciation of the universe; it will stimulate an inner knowledge, giving guidance and direction. It will bring harmony to your life. Meditation is the way to receive and grasp abundant, eternal life.

Those are just the extras. The real gift of meditation is that it offers friendship with Christ . . . and that friendship is the only purpose of meditation. The reign of Christ, the rule of God in the inner kingdom, is enough to make it worth the journey. All the rest that is added is God's gracious generosity.

I wait, then, in the stillness and silence, yearning for the assurance of the divine Mystery. I listen, eager, expectant, for the Voice of the One who called me into being and who is *always* calling me into being together with Him in faithful friendship.

* * *

I rush to make the children's lunches, and there, between sandwiches and raisins, I am struck by the remembrance of the Source of all of life. Even as the sandwiches go in the sacks and the milk money is laid out for rushing hands, His love weaves miraculous bonds of communication among friends.

I see and taste, hear and smell His activity in the extravagance and beauty of nature because I have become sensitive to His presence through meditation. I hear His call in the hurting world and to a particular hurting person, and then I know that the Lord of life has broken through my rush and preoccupation to remind me that He is present and that He is here all the days of my life. He has indeed crashed through my darkness with the Light that never falters. He is risen. He is risen indeed . . . in me.

* * *

The steep mountain path narrowed as my family and I trudged, single file, on above the timberline. We stopped often, filling our

lungs with the thin Colorado air or sharing a grimy tube of Chap-
Stick. The high country was alternately chilly and hot, depending
on the cloud cover, but it was always dry.

"Why are we doing this?" someone would ask, but then we
would spot an even more dazzling field of columbine, Colorado's
state flower, and we would climb a few more feet over the short
grass and rocky mountain.

A gentle group of climbers caught up with us, stopping to
exchange greetings as my children leaned hard into a giant rock.

I couldn't keep from noticing the lack of fear between us, high
up there on the mountainside, and the way we took the time to
look straight into each other's eyes and smile.

"Is this your first time to make the climb?" we asked.

"Oh, no, we've made it many times."

"Is it worth it?" we queried, eyeing the path that wound itself
up the rugged boulders.

"It's worth it!" They all agreed without hesitation.

"Why?" we wanted to know.

"The view . . . the view from the top is spectacular," they
responded, and they went on ahead, urged by the yearning to see
that view from the top again.

A terrible thunderclap shook the nearby heavens, and as the
cold mountain shower moved closer, we had to decide, based on
the word of the others, if the view would be worth the climb and
the risk of being caught in the approaching shower.

We continued to climb. When at last we stood at the top, all
around us was a great stillness, filled with an awesome kind of
grandeur and wonder. Isolated high above the world and far away
from the noise of responsibility, I looked down into a quiet valley
and then around me at the mysteries of the high country and, in
the silence of the mountain, responded to the Source of life.

I felt a surge of peace, as if I were connected to the veteran
climbers, my family, and the world beyond by some bond of love.
I felt full of life and energy and desire. My climb had affirmed the
worth of life.

We would remember the view from the mountain, and the awesome bigness of the valley would forever be impressed upon our

memories. We would carry home the silence of the high country to recollect in the noise of the city.

* * *

Therefore we have been buried with Him through baptism into death, in order that as Christ was raised from the dead through the glory of the Father, so we too might walk in newness of life.
—Romans 6:4

There is a powerful silence of the heart in which there is encounter between creature and Creator; and, indeed, there is a yearning for that encounter and an inner knowing that the view of life from that encounter is spectacular. It is worth the trip through the valleys of darkness to stand, once again, in the Light.

EXERCISE

After you have relaxed and focused on God's presence, sit in the stillness and imagine that Christ is with you.

Picture yourself walking along the sea in the cool of the evening with Jesus. What would you like to tell Him?

Sit in the silence a little longer. See Jesus turn to you. What is He telling you?

He asks you to follow Him. What is your response?

What do you have to lose?

What will you gain?

What do you decide?

NOTES

1. Henri J. M. Nouwen, *With Open Hands* (Notre Dame, IN: Ave Maria Press, 1972).
2. Karl Olsson, *Come to the Party* (Waco, TX: Word Books, 1972).
3. Henri LeSaux, *Prayer* (Philadelphia: Westminster Press), p. 6, as quoted by M. Basil Pennington in *Daily We Touch Him* (Garden City, NY: Doubleday, 1977), p. 79.
4. Elizabeth O'Connor, *Eighth Day of Creation* (Waco, TX: Word Books, 1971).
5. Jeanne Guyon, *Experiencing the Depths of Jesus Christ* (Gardiner, ME: Christian Books, 1980).
6. Francois Fénelon, *Let Go* (Springdale, PA: Whitaker House, 1973).
7. Francois Fénelon, *The Royal Way of the Cross* (Orleans, MA: Rock Harbor Press, 1980), p. 81.
8. Andrew Murray, *The Believer's Secret of Waiting on God* (Minneapolis: Bethany House, 1986).
9. Keith Miller, *The Scent of Love* (Waco, TX: Word Books, 1983).
10. Jeanne Guyon, *Experiencing the Depths of Jesus Christ* (Gardiner, ME: Christian Books, 1980).
11. Oswald Chambers, *My Utmost for His Highest* (New York: Dodd, Mead and Company, 1935), p. 118.